Hell's Belle

Hell's Belle
From a B-17 to Stalag 17B

Based on the Memoirs of William E. Rasmussen

Randall L. Rasmussen

SUNSTONE PRESS

SANTA FE

The cover photograph is a picture of a guard tower at Stalag 17B. Guard towers were located all around the perimeter of the compound. (photograph by Ben H. Phelper)

© 2003 by Randall L. Rasmussen. All Rights Reserved.

No part of this book may be reproduced in any form or by any electronic or mechanical means including information storage and retrieval systems without permission in writing from the publisher, except by a reviewer who may quote brief passages in a review.

Sunstone books may be purchased for educational, business, or sales promotional use. For information please write: Special Markets Department, Sunstone Press, P.O. Box 2321, Santa Fe, New Mexico 87504-2321.

Library of Congress Cataloging-in-Publication Data

Rasmussen, Randall L., 1949-
  Hell's Belle : based on the memoirs of William E. Rasmussen : from a B-17 to Stalag 17B / by Randall L. Rasmussen.
     p. cm.
  ISBN 0-86534-405-1 (pbk.)
   1. Rasmussen, William E. 2. United States. Army Air Forces—Biography. 3. World War, 1939-1945—Personal narratives, American. 4. Prisoners of war—United States—Biography. 5. World War, 1939-1945—Prisoners and prisons, German. 6. Stalag XVII B Krems-Gneixendorf. I. Title.

D811.R324 A3 2003
940.54'7243'092—dc22   2003014064

Published in SUNSTONE PRESS
POST OFFICE BOX 2321
SANTA FE, NM 87504-2321 / USA
(505) 988-4418 / *ORDERS ONLY* (800) 243-5644
FAX (505) 988-1025
WWW.SUNSTONEPRESS.COM

CONTENTS

1 Next Stop Europe............................ 7
2 England 16
3 Aerial Combat 21
4 Bombing 25
5 A New B–17 34
6 Hell's Belle 39
7 Solingen-Leverkunsen 42
8 Capture 52
9 Federal Prison to Dulag Luft 60
10 Dulag Luft to Stalag 17B 72
11 Stalag 17B 80
12 A Notice Home 93
13 Some Grub to Eat 109
14 The Cemetery 114
15 Time For a Prayer 121
16 Camp Life 124
17 The Ninth Life 128
18 The Escape Committee 133

19	*A German Mole*	*139*
20	*Mail Call*	*154*
21	*Show Time*	*158*
22	*Word Home*	*161*
23	*Kick-A-Poo Juice*	*164*
24	*Happy New Year*	*167*
25	*Spring Break*	*170*
26	*Forced March*	*172*
27	*The Way Home*	*187*

Epilogue *198*

About William E. Rasmussen *200*

Appendix I:
The B-17 and the American Flyer *201*

Appendix II: The 8th Airforce
and Daylight Bombing *207*

1

Next Stop Europe

1 AM SEPTEMBER 14, 1943. WE WERE EDGING CLOSER TO battle. Our crew was a replacement outfit for a B-17 that had already been lost over Nazi Germany. We had flown our B-17, the *Anxious Angel*, from Gander, Newfoundland, to Nuts Corner, Northern Ireland. Three days later, four hundred seventy American flyers were shuttled by bus the short distance to Belfast, then on to a ship bound for England.

It was almost midnight when the Irish transport ship set out to sea and the eight-hour passage in the dead of the night. I surveyed the Irish ship; the two hundred foot long craft was lightly armored. It had only two machine gun emplacements, one fore and one aft. The ship was cloaked in black, and left an even darker port behind. All the lights were out in Ireland, as well as England. Night bombing by German bombers had already commenced for the evening. The ship ran stealthily through the night, bearing south, at twelve knots. It was roughly one hundred twenty miles across the Irish Sea to our destination at Liverpool, a port on the west coast of England.

"These waters are infested with Nazi U-boats," one of the rugged Irish sailors reminded us after leaving port in Belfast, several times in fact, in a very convincing voice. The sailor had a pot-marked face and short red hair. In another era he would have made a great pirate. He acted like he was lecturing to a bunch of schoolboys. The Irish sailors were older than the American flyers. He looked all of forty. I was just two weeks shy of my twenty-third birthday. Most of the Irish sailors were bigger than the American flyers as well. Flyers had a size limit in order to fit into the cramped spaces on the B-17. Out at sea, the sailors carried themselves with an air of confidence that the American flyers didn't share. We were, after all, a good bit out of our element. "We've lost numerous ships enroute to Liverpool," he said in his thick Irish accent. I wondered if he talked that way just so we would have to pay closer attention in order to understand him.

Troops were hanging from the yardarms trying to sleep on the deck; others packed into every corner that was big enough to hold a body. Two of the more than one hundred flyers that were topside were Charlie Dyer and myself. We crouched in a niche on some steps. Charlie and I had met during training and had become best friends. He sat down next to me with a very concerned look on his face. "I don't think I'm gonna sleep tonight, Ras," Charlie said. "The Irish are acting as if we're next on the German target list."

Charlie was a soft-spoken, handsome guy, from Spencer, Indiana. Like me, he looked forward to getting done with the week's training and going out for a cold beer at the local pub. Charlie usually wore a smile that made you think he was up to something. Now, in the dead of the night, the dark shadows that were always around his eyes made him look exhausted.

"Well, look at it this way Charlie, if we are torpedoed, then there might still be a chance that we can survive by jumping overboard." I said with a chuckle. Charlie didn't think that was funny. "They're toying with us," I said. "They know we're a bunch of rookies and they're trying to spook us." I wondered why we hadn't departed with more cloud cover. The full moon lit up the ship and it could be seen for several miles. Most of the other American flyers were lost in their private thoughts. Leaving the States and the initial excitement of going to war was beginning to fade into the realization of what was ahead of us. Some of these soldiers would not be going back home.

As we sat there, my thoughts drifted back over the last sixteen months. I had graduated from engineering school at Cal Flyers at Inglewood, California, eleven months earlier and had been assigned to specialty school at the Douglas Aircraft Plant. From there it was on to San Antonio, Texas to be part of a repair squadron at the newly opened Duncan Field. At San Antonio, I flew on a B-25 light bomber on coast patrol around the Gulf of Mexico, looking for submarines.

Two weeks later, I was picked to be part of a salvage crew based in Monterrey, Mexico. The salvage crew was made up of eight men with twelve different aircraft specialties. My specialties were hydraulics and propellers. We were to locate downed cadets and their planes that had flown out of bases in Texas. Our assignment was to determine what mechanical failure had caused the plane to crash. Most of the time the planes had crashed simply because they ran out of gas. By the tenth day of duty as a member of a salvage crew I applied for gunnery school.

"You don't have to convince me how important it is to locate downed cadets," I told my CO. "I'm just not convinced it can't be done without me." Shortly afterwards, I received transfer orders to Laredo Arial Gunnery School (LAGS). At Laredo, the soldiers were screened to be sure they weren't too trigger-happy.

"You will take .30 and .50-caliber machine guns apart, learn their parts and be able to replace them all in working order and do it in a specified time," barked the drill sergeant. The guns were very impressive. They had been developed after WWI and were armor piercing. Five hundred-round, linked ammunition belts fed them. Each round was just over five inches long. The guns were twin mounted in turrets and weighed sixty-four pounds each.

On graduation day from LAGS, two of the officers at school requested that we let them know what they should add to the program to make it more effective. I, for one, did what they requested and managed to end up in the CO's office to explain why I was trying to rearrange the training program.

"All gunners should be provided with silk gloves to wear under our heated gloves so that when they remove the outer pair their hands won't freeze to the cold metal," I told them. "In addition, our chute's harness could be improved. We should incorporate a single release such as the British use and not the series of snap connectors we have. That way, if the flyer is forced to bail out over water, he can extract himself before the silk chute pulls him under. With the single release mechanism, he can turn the lock, hit the button and keep a good hold on the chute shrouds. In so doing, the harness would actually explode, leaving the flyer free to drop the last few feet and swim out from under the falling canopy," I explained to them with a satisfied look on my face.

"Thank you Sergeant," one of the officers replied and held the door open. Neither of them was smiling as I left their office. Despite the brush-off, I felt invincible. I was on top of the world when I got my new assignment. It was a transfer to Moses Lake, Washington to train as a crewmember on a B-17 heavy bomber.

Assignment on the heavy bombers had been just two months before our arrival in Europe. That's where I met Charlie. We trained together at Moses Lake and were assigned to the *Anxious Angel*. The Moses Lake base was actually in the middle of desert. I was assigned to barracks with scores of other GIs, including Charlie, who were all destined to become part of B-17 crews. It was there that I met the other flyers who were assigned to the *Angel*, and were now on the same transport ship that was tiptoeing its way, in the middle of the night, across the Irish Sea.

The *Angel*, like all 17s, had a crew of ten: four officers, Charles Quinn pilot, Ken Falleck co-pilot, Robert Hornbeck navigator and nose gunner, and Sidney Edelstein bombardier and nose gunner, and six sergeants, Harold Wingate top turret gunner who also served as flight engineer, Bert Steiler top hatch gunner and radio operator, Harold McDowell tail gunner trained in armament, two waist gunners, John Hinda trained in armament and Charlie Dyer trained as engineer, and me, Bill Rasmussen ball turret gunner in the belly of the plane, also trained in engineering. Some of us were college boys from small town

America. By war's end we were soldiers and thought of each other as brothers.

"Wingate top turret, Rasmussen ball turret." The colonel barked out our assignment after we arrived at Moses Lake. Wingate was an inch taller and a little heavier than me so he got assigned to the top turret. The smallest guy got the ball turret. At five feet, eight inches, and a hundred and seventy pounds, that was me. The ball turret is a Plexiglas ball, four feet in diameter that hangs from the belly of the B-17. It rotates 360 degrees in flight. Twin .50-caliber Browning machine guns are mounted in the turret. The ball turret gunner has to crawl through a hatch, a little over a foot in diameter, to get into the ball after takeoff and back out before landing. The hatch remains closed, and the gunner inside the turret, during the mission. Once inside, the ball turret gunner's back rests on the back of the Plexiglas ball. The two machine guns straddle his legs. Controls for the machine guns and the electrical motors that operate the turret are located on handgrips.

I looked out at the vacant sea as a large wave hit the side of the ship, spraying salt-water over the deck and momentarily breaking my thoughts. I had never been at sea before and was surprised how the smell of salt water filled the air.

Just four weeks before departing for Ireland, we had been transferred from Moses Lake to Madras, Oregon to train in combat flying. Not everything went smoothly at Madras. "You start with instrument routing and simulated bombing." Major Jack Arnold, the CO at Madras voice echoed back to me. We practiced simulated bombing runs at high altitudes then low altitudes with air—to—ground and air—to—air firing. We drilled with and without staged malfunctions. Then we ran the same routine all over again with the *Angel* in a formation with a number of other 17s.

"The next run will be a simulated mission," the Major announced a week before our departure to Europe. "There will be three checkpoints, then back to base."

Several hours into the run Hornbeck, our navigator, announced, "We're lost! We missed the second checkpoint!"

"The Major's going to be pissed," Quinn, our pilot, said.

After two hours of flying about and still unable to get our bearings Edelstein, our bombardier summed it up, "We're down on fuel and we either gotta find a place to land or ditch the plane and jump."

"There's an airfield with a strip large enough to land our ship," Quinn yelled. Quinn had spotted an airfield that was absent any aircraft. He sat the *Angel* down smoothly and without incident and prepared for the worst.

"Hey, look guys," Falleck our co-pilot was pointing to the edge of the airfield. "Those are B-29s in that hanger." It turned out that we had headed east instead of north from the second marker and landed at a new base at Mount Home, Idaho! It was in a field that was being built for the new B-29 series of aircraft. The two hundred people that were assigned to this location treated us like royal guests.

"I would like to be the fly on the wall when your CO gets you," one of them ribbed us. "You guys are going to catch some hell!" After refueling and an uneventful return flight to the base at Madras, the officers, Quinn, Falleck, Edelstein and Hornbeck were each fined one hundred dollars. It hurt their wallets and hurt their pride as well. Sitting on the deck of the Irish transport ship, I was wondering how we had missed the second checkpoint. Hornbeck had better not miscalculate our flight plan over Nazi Germany.

When orders came to depart Madras for England we flew the *Anxious Angel* to Presque Isle, Maine, our last stop in the States, then on to Gander, Newfoundland, before heading across the Atlantic. Bert Steiler, Charlie and I pooled our money to purchase extra rations, including tomato soup and canned pineapple.

"There's hardly any food left in England," Steiler had declared. "At least we'll have some canned goods to eat. Besides, with everyone going hungry over there, there'll be a nice profit in selling canned stuff."

On September 8, 1943, forty-seven of the heavy bombers left Presque Isle for Gander, Newfoundland. The bombers left Gander at six-minute intervals and took one of four different routes to England. The flight pattern was designed to confuse the German spies. The first plane flew directly to Ireland, the next north to Bluie West I in Greenland, followed by the third plane flying north to Iceland, and the fourth to Bluie West II, Greenland. Then this pattern repeated itself. There was also a southern route to gain access to England from Florida across to the Azores, then to Casablanca and then north to England. But the *Anxious Angel* was not among them. Our departure had been postponed.

"Quinn's got the flu," Hornbeck announced after we arrived at Gander. Three days later he recovered, and we were ordered to take the direct route to Ireland, a trip of about 2,000 miles. On September 11, we flew the *Anxious Angel* across the Atlantic, unaccompanied by any other B-17. Hornbeck hit the runway at Nuts Corner dead on and without any wasted travel time.

"I'm sure glad you learned how to use a compass, Hornbeck," Falleck, our co-pilot, teased when we landed.

We lost the *Angel* at Nuts Corner. Ferry Command confiscated her. It was their job to transport arriving bombers to a repair depot where these ships were outfitted for combat. "The ship has to have additional armor plating," the lieutenant from Ferry Command told us.

"I was beginning to like that ship," Charlie said. "Especially after flying her safely across the Atlantic. Besides, flying with an *Angel* has got be good luck." Charlie's comments echoed what the rest of us were thinking. Crews on the 17s were a superstitious lot and didn't like change. In addition, the *Angel* had the most advanced modifications including a third turret that mounted two .50-caliber Browning machine guns under its chin. Any replacement ship could not be a better one. But, no one from Ferry Command had asked for our opinion.

The opportunity of selling our can goods in England, for a nice profit, never came to be. On arrival at Nuts Corner all the rations were removed from our plane while the crew was at chow. We stayed in there for three restless days, then were transported by bus to the estuary at Belfast.

Charlie and I sat there staring out at the sea. I broke the silence and decided to tell him a story. "Did I tell you the time I was traveling home from college and came across an old preacher I recognized trying to fix a flat on his car?" I asked Charlie. "He had pulled his car, flat and all, along side the road and had a quizzical look on his face as I rode along past him."

"Don't believe you have, Ras," he answered.

"Well, I knew this fellow to be a self ordained reverend, always looking for a flock to follow him. Ran across him just before I was getting into Cedar, to spend the weekend at home, so I stopped to help him. Said he was having a hard time getting his tire off. Apparently the lugs had rusted on the old car."

"You sure enough never told me about this. What happened next?" Charlie asked.

"I told him to try hammering the wrench while it's still on the lugs."

"Tried that," he said.

"Well, then jack up the back of the car and we'll kick it off the jack, that'll loosen 'em," I told the minister.

"Done that already," was his reply.

"Well," I told him. "The only other thing you can do is run the car on the flat. Eventually it has to loosen the lugs."

"Ran it for miles already," he told me.

I figured we had a long night ahead of us so I took my time telling Charlie the rest of the story. Finally Charlie asked, "So, what did you tell him to do, Ras?" By now he was paying close attention to my story.

"Told him he should try practicing what he preached, that it never hurts to turn to prayer in tough times."

"Well, son," he replied. "You may be right. Let's say we offer one up together."

"And?" Charlie said after I paused again.

"And we knelt down and said a prayer, both of us, right there next to the road and in front of his flat tire. Said several prayers in fact. When we were done, I stood up, grabbed the wrench, and the lugs turned off, this time without much effort!"

"Nooooo," Charlie replied. "What did the preacher say to that?"

"Said, 'I'll be dammed!' with quite a look on his face."

Charlie and I must have laughed for the next five minutes.

Charlie looked a good bit better during the rest of the journey. It was almost 3 AM and cold on deck. It is always colder out on the sea than in the port. We were buffered from the cold with our thick fleece-lined flyer's jackets. The only noise on deck was the low rumble of the ship's diesel engines as it made its journey south. Charlie fell asleep.

I sat there thinking that I should be back in college. It had been five years since I had entered Central Michigan Teacher's College at Mt. Pleasant, Michigan. At the time, I had a total accumulated savings of $25. Tuition was $18.75 per term so I had a few dollars left to find a room that cost $2.50 per week. I picked geology and geography as majors and had a part-time job playing the trumpet three nights a week at the Clare Country Club. Those were the days, I thought. The band played Dixie. The ladies put their heads on their partner's shoulder and smiled while they danced the night away. It always made me feel good to think that my music made other people feel so happy. Sometimes I played Henry Busse's *Hot Lips,* everyone's favorite, or muted my trumpet, and played Clyde McCoy's *Sugar Blues.* I was on top of the world, and I was on my way.

The moon lit a white path across the top of the sea. Within the hour the lit path drifted along the ship's starboard side and settled near the rear of the Irish ship as it turned from south to southeast towards Liverpool. I sat there on deck the entire night waiting for dawn and watching that moonlit path for a periscope.

2

England

THE IRISH SHIP DOCKED AT LIVERPOOL SHORTLY AFTER DAWN. I thought we might be transported to a barracks for rest. Instead, we were shuttled to a marshalling yard and placed on a train for the one hundred seventy mile ride to Watford, northwest of London.

"Tomorrow you start with aircraft identification training," the lieutenant informed the tired flyers on arrival at Watford.

It was the second time that we were put through aircraft identification training. There, in a classroom, we were shown pictures of allied aircraft and enemy aircraft first for a few seconds then for shorter times, at close distance then at greater distances, until we could tell friend from foe. Then we had to identify aircraft approaching from different angles, in different formations and in differing numbers, first a good look, then just a glimpse. A lot of our planes were mixed up with German aircraft as well.

"The Brits must really be spooked that we're gonna shoot their planes down," Charlie said. We had gone back to our barracks after dinner and were settling in for a game of poker. "I've seen more pictures of British Spitfires than I ever want to see again." The RAF planes looked quite similar to Luftwaffe planes and many had been shot at by

American flyers. It wasn't making for good working relationships with our British allies.

"My deal," I said. "We're playing 'Ol' Ras wins.'" Whenever I'd deal, we played 'Business,' a 7-card stud game that splits the pot with the high spade. It made everyone mad because following my pronouncement I almost always won the pot!

"Where'd you learn how to play?" Charlie asked.

"From my older brother, Harry. We got some of the boys together a few times each summer. Played penny-ante. Harry greeted all our guests with the same invitation. 'Welcome to Ras's Casino where big men bullshit but money talks!'"

By the time we were done with recognition training this time, I didn't think it was possible to mistakenly shoot any aircraft of ours or for that matter RAF planes. Within the week, transfer orders came to relocate us from Watford to our permanent assignment, the airbase at Bassingbourn.

Bassingbourn is forty-five miles north of London and just south of Cambridge. There our crew was assigned to the 401st Bombardment Squadron of the 91st Bombardment Group, in the 1st Wing, of the 8th Air Force. What I did not know then was how vital a role the 91st played in the Allied aerial campaign during WWII. What the 91st Bombardment Group accomplished is a matter of record. By war's end the 91st had flown a total of three hundred forty missions and dropped 22,142 tons of bombs. It was the first group to complete one hundred missions. The 91st destroyed more enemy aircraft than any other group in the entire 8th Air Force, four hundred twenty. The 91st received two Distinguished Unit Citations for achievements on missions to Hamm, Germany on March 4, 1943 and Oschersleben, Germany on January 11, 1944. It was the 91st that led two famous missions against the ball bearing works at Schweinfurt, and Regensburg, Germany on August 17 and October 14, 1943. The *Memphis Belle,* a ship in the 91st, was the first B-17 to complete twenty-five missions without a casualty.

The 91st also suffered grievously. It lost more B-17 Flying Fortresses than any other group, one hundred ninety-seven. The 91st also lost nine hundred one men, and at war's end had another two hundred thirty-three missing and presumed dead. Nine hundred fifty-seven flyers from the 91st became POWs.

The American 8th Air Force flew from the southeast shoulder of England. This small area, forty miles long and eighty miles wide, was home to one hundred twenty-two airbases used for command, bomber and fighter bases. Bassingbourn Airfield was also a permanent base for the English fliers. It was a favorite target for German bombers and there were air raids constantly.

Knowledge of the activity at Bassingbourn became a focus of German interrogation of American flyers after they were captured. If the Germans found out how the B-17s arrived at the airfield, they thought they could identify a target and destroy the pipeline of heavy bombers. Some of my co-prisoners did not return from interrogation. For the obvious reason that some of us would become eventual POWs and because there was no need to know, the source of American bombers was never explained to the flyers. All we knew was that whenever 17s did not return from a bombing raid, replacement 17s were on the runway the next morning. The Germans never accepted that the captured American flyers did not have any idea how the flow of the replacement B-17s could be interrupted.

Bassingbourn was known to our flyers as the "Savoy of the Eighth," all in all, not a bad place to live army life. The barracks were shaped like an "H" and were made of brick, in direct contrast to the Quonset type housing we used elsewhere in England. The buildings were more like our facilities at home. There were tiled bathrooms and regular sidewalks. The food was pretty good too. The base was only a few miles from town where the flyers could go to the local pub for a brew.

The first few hours at our new home were taken up with the usual: finding our quarters, locating the mess hall, briefing rooms and the armament building where each crewmember had to clean, store and oil gun barrels. We found the bay where our newly assigned plane the *"079" Buccaneer* was parked.

What I didn't realize at first was what lay lurking less than a hundred miles east of where I stood. The war was evident everywhere we looked.

"Can you believe what we're looking at?" I asked Charlie the first time we saw actual damage from bombing; an industrial block had been totally leveled. Occasional chimneys stood as the sole survivors of the incendiary bombs. Devastated areas were all around. Air raid sirens sounded every night. The stark reality of war was sinking in. The first letter I received from home wished me safe flying and said how glad I should be to be so far from German entrenchments. By the time that letter reached me, thousands of civilians had already died in England due to bombing, strafing and resulting fires from incendiary bombs.

"It's looks different than the pictures in the paper back home," Charlie said. "Now it really puts me on edge whenever the air sirens go off. I didn't feel that way before we got here."

"Flying weather missions will be part of your orientation," the officer in charge said at our first briefing. We had arrived at Bassingbourn at six o'clock in the morning. The Air Force wasn't inclined to have the crews who had just arrived go immediately into battle. There was a lot to learn about operations at the airfield, navigation in the area and what the Air Force expected of us. Each mission was rather short. We flew out of Bassingbourn at various times and usually returned within four hours. Our assignments were to all points of the compass, north over Scotland, south over the English Channel, east over the North Sea and west over Ireland. After returning to base, we assembled in briefing rooms to give report and ask questions. Fifteen weather missions and two air sea rescue searches later the Commander had new instructions.

"You flyers have completed your orientation," he said. "Your next mission will be a bombing run. Keep a close watch on your barrack's bulletin board for your crew's listing, time of briefing and departure. Also, you are required to check to make certain whether or not you have been picked individually to fly with another crew."

Being named to fly with another crew meant that a flyer had been killed or wounded in battle. This type of situation was quite frequent due to the lack of trained crews that were available late in 1943. At the time of our arrival, planes were more abundant than the crews needed to fly them.

The *"079" Buccaneer's* first notification for a bombing assignment was coming very soon.

3

Combat

ACTIVE DUTY IS ALL THE TIME SERVED WHILE IN UNIFORM, training, inspections, travel, waiting, menial tasks. The call to combat duty is the culmination of military obligations and is the only real purpose for active duty. Our armed services have but two major purposes: one protective, a deterrent to prevent attack on our nation; the other offensive, a war machine whose function is to preserve the safety of our country and that of our allies by destroying the enemy. In WWII there were no halfway solutions, no option for anything other than a complete victory. We had to destroy the enemy so there could be no possibility of conquering the United States. The enemy had to surrender unconditionally. The debates about this conflict had ended. Americans had melted together in their cause. The only two options remaining were to win the war, or be conquered by the Axis. The Axis had to be defeated in combat. The Axis had to suffer total defeat and humiliation because they chose to wage war on America.

  The military teaches discipline. When America was attacked at Pearl Harbor isolationism ended; the recruiting stations filled with excited and cocky young men, eager to join and fight. For these new GIs it was an enthusiastic end to watching the war from the sidelines and a jump-start into battle.

Standing at the recruiting station in Detroit, we recruits felt there were just too many Americans joining the service to think that anything could happen to us. Most of us felt we just needed a rifle in our hands or a tank to drive and we could march right into Berlin, in no time. I doubt any of us understood how strong and how effective denial of getting seriously injured could be. I doubt any one of us knew we were projecting our possible injuries onto someone else as a defense mechanism, guarding against reality. Certainly at that time, none of us thought about becoming a prisoner of war.

"Fighting's gonna be fun," was the feeling echoed by a lot of the recruits. The thought of Germans and Japanese creating carnage of whole countries and genocide was not in our minds.

"You afraid you might get hurt?" I overheard two of the recruits talking in line next to me. None of us thought of losing an arm or a leg or our vision. No one thought about getting burned or even paralyzed.

"No way," the other answered. Each recruit was convinced that nothing bad would happen to him.

The army changed that way of thinking. It was just a matter of time in the service before reality sank in, reality of what your capabilities were, especially with specialized training. The slow, methodical way the military has of making you accountable for the specialized tasks you were trained for, and their uncompromising expectations forced you to perform or be demoted, perform or lose your rank and position that you were selected and had trained for. The military was not about to take excuses for things that went wrong and was not inclined to give many second chances. Everything was expected to go without a glitch; if it didn't, someone was responsible. If you were on a B-17 over Europe in 1943, you could not afford to have anything go wrong.

Devastation has a way of changing your thinking too. What affected me most was the thought of burned flyers. Nothing scared me more than being burned. When a flyer was burned, the pain was enormous and the scarring never healed. If the burns were bad enough, flyers died. They died from infection. It took days for them to die, all of which they suffered in pain.

"Look at that," I said to Charlie. We were standing on the edge of the airfield, when a damaged B-17 that had limped its way back to Bassingbourn crash-landed and burned. Being trapped in the belly turret at the time a B-17 hit the runway without landing gear, skidded, and then burst into flames was something I dreaded. "I'm not going to burn," I told Dyer. The ball turret gunner entered the turret after the bomber was in full flight. The turret rotated 360 degrees underneath the ship and turned minus 90 degrees in elevation, with the guns and the ball turret gunner facing straight down. The turret had to be aligned in the neutral azimuth position with the guns horizontal, pointing straight back, in order to open its door and the gunner crawl back out into the fuselage before landing. The turret operated hydraulically, on pressure built up by the constant speed of an electrical motor. If hydraulic or electrical power were out, the turret froze out of the neutral position and the gunner was trapped in the turret. "If we're going to crash and I'm in the turret, then I want you to shoot me," I told Charlie. Our eyes were glued on the B-17 being eaten by fire. It was my way of dealing with the fear of burning.

"No problem, Ras, be glad to," Dyer said with a grin on his face. "Can do it earlier if you want! In fact, if you tell me any more of your stories I might just shoot you for the fun of it!" Charlie replied.

If you were responsible for something in the military, then you were given authority over it. Each soldier was made to understand his responsibilities and expected to exercise his authority. The military made it very clear what you were in charge of and therefore responsible for. Each flyer had specific duties and no one else was going to fill in, not on a B-17. You could not get a replacement after leaving Bassingbourn. Each flyer had to know what he was doing and be able to execute it over and over again, in a very methodical, precise fashion, and make no mistakes. You had to play it by the book, everything by the numbers as you were taught. The difficult task had to seem easy.

Something that first looked exciting had to become monotonous, even mundane.

The pilot and co-pilot had their special skills. They were under specific instructions to enter formation, fly to the specific target and back home. The navigator could make no mistakes; he had to know alternate evacuation routes in case the 17 was damaged, including flying to Switzerland or across the Mediterranean Sea. The bombardier took over the mission as we approached the target for the bombing run then returned control to the pilot after the payload was dropped. The gunners fought in a battleground five miles above the earth with the German fighters. The crew worked together as a team in an unpressurized cabin, fifty degrees below zero, 27,000 feet above the earth. Nothing worked unless it worked as a whole. A weak link could spell disaster. Everyone understood this and no one tolerated anything from the other crewmembers that interfered with carrying out their responsibilities. There could be no cowboys and no mistakes on a B-17 heavy bomber over Nazi occupied Europe.

The army also taught loyalty. The foot soldiers refer to it as the last man out of the foxhole. When it comes down to it, the instinct for survival can be a difficult one to resist when the going gets tough. It is an instinct that protects oneself but puts the rest of the soldiers at more risk. There is no place to hide on a B-17, no foxhole to crawl out of. You either made it, or all went down together. If you went down, then there was a good chance the entire crew would die in the crash.

Crews normally were not broken up, and that's the way they preferred it. Maybe a little of that was superstition, but a lot of it was the molding together as a crew and the knowledge and trust we had of each other. Each man understood his responsibility and fulfilled his duties. The crew had been through training and orientation flights together and was about to go on combat missions together. The flyers wanted to keep it that way.

4

Bombing

THE CREW OF THE *"079" BUCCANEER* WAITED FOR THEIR assignment. On October 20, 1943 our ship's name was posted on the barrack's bulletin board. Briefing was scheduled at six o'clock the following morning. The posting created an uneasy feeling and apprehension with our crew. The waiting was over. All the preparations were behind us. Tomorrow would bring the first true test of our crew and craft. If there was anything left to learn it would have to be learned in combat.

October 21 started at five o'clock at the latrine hut for a shower and shave. A one or two day old beard had to go because it caused the oxygen mask to leak. Charlie was still shaving and talking to anyone who would listen.

"At least we get real eggs today instead of that powdered crap," he said. "I can't stand those fake eggs." Only on the days they were assigned a mission did the flyers get real eggs.

"I'm sticking with coffee and a slice of buttered toast," I told him. I always waited until we got back to eat a meal.

After hitting the mess hall, it was on to the briefing center. Military police guarded the door. No one entered the room and no one left it during the briefing. In our first briefing, and all subsequent ones, we were glued to every word. Weather conditions over the coast and over the target were forecasted. The rendezvous point for our squadron, somewhere over the North Sea, was assigned. The number of B-17s assigned to the mission and the squadrons comprising the combat wing were detailed. Each crew was instructed on where its squadron was suppose to join the formation and the position in the squadron that their ship was to assume. We were notified what our primary objective was and the route and altitude that our ship was to take. A secondary target was assigned in case the primary one was missed. If the formation was to have fighter escort, the number, type of fighters, and the part of the mission they would be available was disclosed. We always welcomed "our little friends," the P-38s, to join us. Command also provided an estimate of German anti-aircraft artillery fire (flak) and the number, type of fighters, and the part of the mission where German fighters would be encountered. We were also informed if our ship had been picked to be part of a diversionary group.

I had just turned twenty-three the first time the *Buccaneer* was given targets deep inside German held territory. Our first bombing mission was to destroy a uranium mine in Norway. The *Buccaneer* was one of two hundred fifty B-17s assigned to the primary target. After briefing we paid a visit to our chaplain. Everyone flying in combat for the first time was afraid and wanted a last minute word with him.

"Our crew and ship are too good," I told the chaplain. "It won't be our number that comes up, not today anyway." I was trying not to act afraid. On any given day a number of ships did not come back. "We're not going to be left behind," I told him. In reality, you had to be a quick study, or you didn't come back. Every day new ships were on the runway to replace those planes that had been shot down. A steady stream of new crews followed the path to Bassingbourn just like we had. Ever so silently after returning to base, the fear of flying the next mission crept in. Ever so slowly you realized your "fortress" could be penetrated. The chaplain had seen a lot of flyers like me. He listened patiently to what was said.

"Let us pray," he said at our conclusion, then led us in prayers. After prayers, we left for the runway. Time spent with the chaplain became more important with each successive mission.

Our first mission started badly and ended badly. If Goering had been watching he'd have been convinced that the Luftwaffe would win the air war. Our bombers ended up looking like a dog and pony show. On the morning of October 21st the runway had fog so thick it could be cut with a knife. Positioning the aircraft on the runway for takeoff was an experience in itself. If we failed to take off, our ship and crew would be at the mercy of the next craft as it roared down the runway on a blind takeoff and in radio silence. Once airborne, Quinn had the long and tedious task of forming, locating our position in the formation with all the other planes and proceeding to the predetermined target. We flew northeast toward a beacon and arrived at the same time as many other squadrons. Forming two hundred sixty aircraft in weather conditions that were far from ideal took a long time. On this, our first mission, it took too long.

"I can't believe my eyes," Falleck said. The sky was full of B-17s flying in from different bases, from different directions and at varying altitudes. "This looks like a flying circus." By the time we were able to fly in formation, some two hours later, most of the ships did not have enough fuel to complete their mission. The entire formation was called back ostensibly because there were Norwegians in the mines and not just Germans. In reality the mission could not have been completed because of the lack of appropriate planning.

"Oh boy, if this is the way it always is, its no wonder so many of our ships don't come back," I told Charlie when were getting off the plane.

Every third day we were eligible to fly, but it wasn't until five days later that we were back in the sky. Our second assignment was the Daimler-Benz factories in Stuttgart, Germany, factories used by the Axis to produce heavy armament. I lowered myself into the turret shortly after we were airborne, fastened my seatbelt and shoulder straps and secured the hatch. Then it was the usual routine to ready the turret for battle. Azimuth power clutch engaged. Toggle switch flipped to turn the turret's main power on. Sight switch to on. Rheostat adjusted to tune the brightness of the light on the sight. Handgrips to neutral position. The turret moved to the right by pressing the handgrips to the left and moved to the left by pressing them to the right. Pulling back on the handgrips tilted the turret up, press forward and the turret rotated forward, and the guns pointed down. Press all the way forward and the guns pointed straight down. There were no safety switches and no triggers to pull. The Brownings fired by pressing firing buttons, one for each gun located on top of the respective handgrip.

"Clear your guns," Quinn ordered at 10,000 feet. Condensation can freeze inside the machine guns as the aircraft ascends to cruising altitude of 27,000 feet. A burst of fire allowed a lubricant to keep the guns from becoming inoperative. The ammunition belt fed tracer rounds every fifth cartridge that could be seen falling across the horizon.

Formation went without a glitch. We were on course and flying at 27,000 feet when we were again called back because of fuel problems with a number of the other ships. Returning to base was easier to accept the second time because, to this point, the mission was much more professionally carried out. The order given had been given as a precaution to get as many B-17s as possible back to Bassingbourn and not jeopardize the ships and crew simply because of low fuel.

"The problem with not completing the mission," Quinn chattered into the mike on the way back, "is that it doesn't count for the required number to fulfill our combat obligation." Unless you made it to the target and dropped your bomb load the mission didn't count.

We were back in the sky two days later. Our target was a marshalling yard in Bremen, Germany, just south of the Danish border. The *Buccaneer* was loaded with sixteen, five hundred-pound high demolition bombs, hung from shackles. We weren't about to let high demolition bombs fall off during flight, so we attached them to the shackles with bailing wire. We removed the wire before we went into the bombing run. It wasn't regulation. On other missions we carried incendiary bombs, all intended to go off on impact. The October 28th raid was the first one thousand-plane mission by B-17s into Nazi Germany. The 8th Air Force was earning its stripes, a thousand warships all carrying high demolition and incendiary bombs. The formation flew in a vertical wedge protecting it from the German Messerschmitts.

It was there that we got our first experience in concentrated antiaircraft artillery bursts. At two o'clock high, the shell had exploded on our starboard side above the ship. Quinn lowered the elevation of the ship and drifted in the port direction. But if the shell exploded underneath us, Quinn was blind to it. As I rotated in the ball turret in the belly of the *Buccaneer*, I could sometimes help him identify where the burst of flak came from and where the white smoke of the flak was relative to our position.

"Eight o'clock low, Quinn," I barked into the mike. The shell exploded underneath us on the port side. Quinn elevated the ship and moved in the starboard direction.

"No wonder they got a bead on us," Charlie said. "Look at those spotter planes." The Germans did their part by having spotter planes calling to their ground forces our exact altitude and air speed. They flew to the side of our formation and out of range of our Brownings.

"At least the flak's not too accurate when we're this high," Steiler said. The flak rose as high as 40,000 feet, although it lost a lot of accuracy above 15,000 feet.

When we were under attack with antiaircraft artillery the Messerschmitts were nowhere to be seen. When the flak stopped the air battle with the German fighters began. Between the flak and the German fighters the sunny blue skies over Germany turned into a five-mile high battleground and a fight to the death.

"Charlie," I yelled into my mike. "Charlie, I'm out of ammo." My Brownings had gone silent. Built into the top of the Sperry turret were two ammunition cans, one for each gun, covered by a plate held in place by four fasteners. Each can had baffle plates to insure positive feeding and to keep the five hundred rounds from tumbling about. I loaded the cans preflight and fed the chutes into the feedways of the guns. During

29

flight, the waist gunner had to replenish the ammunition from the outside of the turret.

McDowell, our tail gunner spotted them first. "Look behind us," he said. Two B-17s had exploded in midair, hit by flak in their fuel tanks or worse, their bombs. Messerschmitts fell too, hit by the thousands of rounds of ammunition fired from the B-17s.

After returning to base we learned that intelligence had picked up movement of heavy equipment and troop columns behind enemy lines in France and the Netherlands. Three days passed and the *Buccaneer* was again posted on the bulletin board.

"The enemy has left themselves vulnerable for bombing attacks and we have been ordered to take full advantage of it," the colonel said at briefing. Raids inside Germany would have to wait until every opportunity to destroy troop trains and hubs of transportation for the German military was exhausted. "Expect to fly every three to five days. Consider yourselves part of a rapid strike force, quick in, drop your payload over the specified target and get out."

Each mission brought a new primary assignment, troop trains outside Rotterdam, and a munitions dump outside Leeuwarden in the Netherlands, a new airbase near Le Harve, and a submarine base at St. Malo in France. The routine for each of the missions was the same. We left at dawn, formed over the North Sea, dropped down on our targets, released our payload, then ran for our lives. When we formed, the sun was climbing over the eastern horizon. All along the coast the Germans had antiaircraft artillery to greet us. The limited range of these missions allowed P-38 fighters to accompany us, making these sorties eminently safer than our raids over Germany. After the mission to St. Malo we were back on base by noon when we learned that the brass had given us a week's reprieve.

"I'm glad that's it for a while," Charlie said. With four missions in less than three weeks, I feel like we're testing our luck."

On November 25, 1943 the *Buccaneer*'s name was again posted. At briefing we were told that our primary target was a munitions factory at Bremen. At first the sheer fascination of flying on a B-17 heavy bomber had been overwhelming. Seeing other ships flying side by side with ours always captured my attention. Seeing a thousand battle ships forming over the North Sea was spellbinding. The wedge passed through a heavy barrage of flak.

"Jesus," Charlie said. "That was close, Quinn." Charlie yelled into the mike. An antiaircraft shell had exploded directly in our flight path. The close burst of flak sent shrapnel through the Buccaneer's skin. Speckles of light could be seen next to where the waste gunner stood.

We were preparing to engage German fighters when a B-17 surfaced from nowhere. "Climb Quinn, climb!" I screamed into the mike. Before Quinn could react the 17 rammed into our port wing, its propeller gnawing a long bite out of the *Buccaneer*'s wing. The 17 that rammed us had come and gone in a matter of seconds. I had felt the other ship as it rose next to my belly turret. The *Buccaneer* shuddered when it was rammed and momentarily veered off its flight path. A chill went down my spine. I thought we might plummet to earth.

"What was that?" It was Quinn's turn on the mike.

"We've been rammed by another 17," I yelled. "One of its propellers has just chewed a large piece out of our left wing."

"How bad's it look?" Quinn asked.

"I don't know," I answered, surveying the damage from my position under the ship. "It don't look good, that's for sure. We're missin' a good fifteen to twenty foot hunk of the wing." Everyone else was silent waiting to hear my damage assessment "The aileron and flaps are gone. There's hydraulic fuel leaking. I don't see any cracks but that doesn't mean there aren't any. I'm not certain she'll hold together, Quinn."

After a short pause Quinn announced, "We're staying with the formation. There's no fire. The controls all respond." We managed to stay in the wedge and fly to our designated target. As I spun around inside the turret firing at German Messerschmitts, I couldn't help but keep glancing up at the damaged wing wondering how long it would stay together and if the *Buccaneer* had enough hydraulic fuel to stay in formation, get to our target and back home safely to Bassingbourn. Our only other choice was to leave formation and make a run for it.

But, the chance of one damaged 17 flying back to Bassingbourn was null.

The wedge dropped to 10,000 feet when we arrived at Bremen, slowed to 155 MPH and went into bombing formation. "The bomb bay doors won't open," shouted Edelstein. "They're not budging! Steiler and Wingate," Edelstein barked to our radio operator and top turret gunner, "force the doors open and push 'em out!"

On the B-17, the tail gunner, waist gunners, and ball turret gunner are all in the fuselage; the radio room is in front of the fuselage and the bomb bay is in front of the radio room. A narrow metal catwalk is the only way to cross the bomb bay and reach the forward compartments, the bridge and the cone. The catwalk hangs from medal supports riveted to the top of the ship. The pilot and copilot are up top, in the bridge, just in front of the bomb bay. Edelstein, the bombardier, Hornbeck, our navigator and Wingate, the top turret gunner, all had to go through a crawl space underneath the bridge to get to the cone.

The bombs hung on rotating shackles along the outer sides of the ship, immediately above the bomb bay doors. Steiler and Wingate turned hand cranks to open the large medal doors, each ten feet long and six feet wide. Both flyers stood sideways on the catwalk as the bombs were released. Ten thousand feet below the open bomb bay doors was the munitions factory. Despite its damage, the *Buccaneer* completed its mission and stayed with the formation as it made its way back to Bassingbourn.

"Buckle up," Quinn ordered on return. McDowell, Hinda, Steiler, Charlie and myself were in the fuselage. The flight crew and Wingate were in the forward compartments. Quinn radioed the flight tower at Bassingbourn, "We're coming in hot." Damaged craft and those with wounded on board were given priority clearance to land.

"I could hardly tell when the tires met good old terra firma," Charlie said once we were back at the mess hall. It was a testimony to the B-17's battle worthiness.

"Yep. You know something, Charlie, I think that's a hell of a start for our war," I reminisced once we had a chance to relax. "On our first mission we almost collide with any one of a hundred of our ships and get called back to base. The next time up everybody runs out of fuel and we get called back. Then on our sixth mission you almost get your butt shot off and we're able to drop our bombs only after one of our own planes practically takes us out of the air!"

"I can hardly wait to see what's next," Charlie said quietly.

The *"079" Buccaneer* was classified as lost.

5

A New B-17

B-17S KEPT ROLLING OFF BOEING'S AND DOUGLAS'S FACTORY lines and rushed to Bassingbourn. When America entered the war the United States Air Force had 3,305 aircraft ready for service and the Navy another 3,000. In 1942 American aeronautical industry turned out 10,769 fighters and 12,627 bombers, more than sixty a day. In 1943 that number grew to 23,988 fighters and 29,355 bombers, nearly one hundred fifty a day.

The 91st lost no time in assigning our crew another B-17, an old one. The *Hell's Belle* had been transferred from the 385th to the 401st Bombardment Group. After the briefing, we walked from the command center to the runway to look at our new craft.

"It looks like an old workhorse that should be put out to pasture," I said after the first glance at the *Belle*. The *Belle* was a 17-F without the chin turret that was on the newer 17-G.

"That's some replacement ship," Steiler muttered. "How come we don't get a new one?" None of us had anything good to say about it. Then we noticed the marks from thirty missions under the pilot's window and patches over the shrapnel and machine gun holes along her sides. With all of those markings and all those patched holes the *Belle* looked as if she couldn't be killed. We stood there for a moment, staring at her, before sharing our thoughts.

"I wonder what it was like for this ship and her crew to have flown thirty missions," Charlie mused. "She's been through a lot. Wonder what hat happened to her crew? Do you think they got assigned stateside or if some of them didn't make it? Looks like she took a lot of hits."

The *Belle* was a battle-hardened ship and had a presence that was quite different than the *Buccaneer*. As our crew silently walked away from the *Belle,* a strange feeling came over me. I felt that we were being watched and our capabilities as a crew were being evaluated. I felt the Belle was questioning our worthiness to be her crew. As we were leaving I looked back at her and swore that the *Belle* caught me in her glare.

The Germans were in for a rude awakening on the morning of November 29. Four hundred B-17s formed over the North Sea without a glitch, the *Hell's Belle* among them, out of range of enemy fighters. The formation held together flawlessly in a vertical wedge. The wedge flew east to the Frisian Islands just off the coast, north of the Netherlands. We nicknamed the Frisian Islands "flak islands" because of the heavy concentration of artillery and their ability to put a screen of exploding shells from the antiaircraft artillery in, about, behind, and in front of us. Flying over the Frisians was like dancing on a rug of 88 rounds. Just past the border of the Netherlands with Germany we dove south towards the Fatherland. As the formation passed over the continent we were again favored by the attention of "Goering's Boys." The formation was under heavy attack from the German fighters when our P-47 Thunderbolts arrived and routed the German Bf-109s. The Thunderbolts were not able to stay long but had done a superb job. The wing gasoline tank for fighters was still experimental and the range of our fighters was limited compared to the heavy bombers. Then, at a given point in the mission, the main group turned east. Three hundred eighty-eight B-17s flew in tight formation, and prepared to bomb the primary target, a marshalling yard outside of Hamburg.

The *Belle* had been selected as part of a diversionary group of 17s and was assigned the lowest position in the group. Two squadrons, twelve B-17s, left the main formation and turned directly south toward Bremen and a ball bearing factory. Ball bearings reduce friction in a rotating shaft where the moving and stationary parts are separated by the metal balls that revolve freely in a lubricated track. Ball bearings allow turrets to rotate and tanks to roll. Ball bearing factories were prime targets of the 91st in order to help cripple the German's ability to wage war.

In theory, the diversionary group was supposed to draw the enemy fighter's attention, leaving the main force with fewer Messerschmitts to deal with. In realty, the diversionary plan didn't confuse the German command very much. The German radar system and spotter planes were able to track the main force, and at the same time have additional fighters engage the diversionary group. Banking south and accelerating, the *Belle* seemed to know her way toward Bremen, her four 1200-HP Wright engines running at full throttle.

German Messerschmitt 110s were on us shortly after we left the main wedge. The Me-110 was powered by two 1,475-HP Daimler-Benz engines and had an operating radius of 1,305 miles with an extra fuel tank. It had a crew of two. Its armament consisted of four 7.9 mm MG 17 machine guns, two MG 81Z machine guns and two 20 mm MG 151 cannons. The *Belle* and the other 17s in the diversionary group were racing at battle speed, trying to outrun the German fighters at speeds in excess of 300 MPH. But, German engineering had given the Luftwaffe what they needed in a fighter: fast, maneuverable and accurate. The Me 110G-4 was capable of attacking the 17s at almost any altitude. It had a maximum speed of 342 MPH at 22,900 feet. Still, twelve B-17s could hold their own against any group of fighters. On November 29, 1943, the new crew of the *Hell's Belle* was in a major air battle. On that day we were outnumbered, but not outgunned.

"They're coming in from the front," Wingate said. "Three of them at one o'clock level." If the fighters came in nose first the speed of the two planes approaching each other gave only one opportunity to fire one quick machine gun burst. The Brownings fired eight hundred forty rounds per minute; fourteen rounds a second. The heavy guns recoiled with each round fired. Maximum range was four miles. At close distances the half-inch wide cartridge wrecked anything in its way. It pierced a plate of armor a half inch thick. At four miles it would still kill a man.

"Ras, three of them at nine o'clock," Charlie shouted. If they came first from the sides or from the tail you got three or four bursts at them.

November 29 was my first confirmed "kill" of an enemy fighter in an air battle, and I caused damage to several others. The Messerschmitt was approaching from our starboard side, guns blazing. It fired several rounds that pierced our fuselage. I trained my dual .50-caliber machine guns on the nose of the fighter, steadying my hand on the firing buttons, and before it had time to veer off, it just came apart four hundred yards off our starboard bow. I had hit other fighters in combat but none had been so close to our ship nor come apart. An image of our own 17s exploding flashed through my mind. At Bremen the diversionary group went into bombing formation, dropped their payload, then turned north and fought their way back over the Netherlands and back over the North Sea.

"There goes another 17," McDowell said, as another in our diversionary group went down, a victim of flak. The shock of seeing other B-17s being shot down was a bitter pill to swallow. We were still a long way from our home base. We had to ration our ammunition and keep the menacing fighters aware that we were still watching their every move. As we approached the northern border of Holland the eight remaining 17s flew through an area where flak peppered the sky.

"Look what's headed our way," Quinn said as we approached the North Sea. P-51 Mustangs met us. I don't believe I was ever so glad to see our fighters.

"I swear that the Messerschmitts were taking aim on the ball turret," I told the rest of our crew after the German fighters broke off.

"Me too, McDowell, the tail gunner said. The rest if the crew felt that the anti-aircraft guns were zeroing in on them as well.

"So did I," Wingate, our top turret operator, said.

Edelstein, our bombardier, and Hornbeck, our navigator, were convinced they were the intended targets. It made for lots of conversation as the remaining ships worked their way back home.

John Hinda, our right waist gunner suffered frostbite on one ear on the mission. Flying at 27,000 feet, with a wind chill factor of fifty degrees below zero, Hinda became a victim of the cold. Command would have to assign the *Belle* a new waist gunner.

"We're not going to make it through too many missions as part of the diversionary group," Charlie said when we were getting off the *Belle*.

"Let's meet back at the compound, Charlie. We'll get a beer."

I was the last member of the crew to leave the plane. The contents of my escape kit had been scattered about and I wanted to put them back in order. As I was walking away there was a long groaning sound that came from the ship. I turned around and stared at the *Belle*. The sound had not come from the engines and could not have come from the stationary fuselage.

"There's something about that ship," I told Charlie when we got to the pub.

"What do you mean?" he asked.

"I get the feeling that it's trying to tell me something. When I left her this afternoon, the same strange feeling came over me that I had when we first went to check her out."

"The only thing strange around here is you, Ras," Charlie said. "Kill your beer and let's go." We downed our suds and headed back to quarters for some much-deserved rest.

6

Hell's Belle

AT NIGHT THE *BELLE* KEPT VIGIL ON THE RUNWAY, NEVER afraid of being outside or alone. *Belle* never got cold despite the freezing temperature. Her skin was too thick and was impervious to snow and rain. If she slept, it was ever so lightly, waiting to take her crew on their next mission. *Belle* opened her eyes when we approached and we never left her gaze until each crewmember was onboard. Her eyes never blinked when she stared at us. They were neither happy nor sad; rather, they looked straight through each of us.

Today we were again assigned to fly the *Hell's Belle*, or more correctly with her. We didn't fly the *Belle*; she flew herself. *Belle* knew where to go and how to get back to Bassingbourn. *Belle* went beyond pride. If she had any emotion, it was loyalty. Her purpose was to conduct us safely on our mission and back home. She asked for nothing in return.

Belle wasn't friendly to anyone, except in a certain manner to us, her crew. Even with her crew she didn't speak. She did not even acknowledge us as we approached on the runway. She only stared with those piercing eyes. With her payload of 8,000 pounds of bombs she bore the weight of each crewmember as he climbed onboard counting as we boarded, pilot, co-pilot, navigator, bombardier, top turret gunner, radio operator, the waist gunners, tail gunner, and me, the gunner in the belly turret. *Belle* counted again when we got back to be sure we had all survived the mission.

Stepping into the fuselage, I patted her side. "Good morning, *Belle*," I said, trying to be friendly.

Belle waited as we strapped in and went through our checklist, then beckoned us to silence when the switch was flipped and her 1,200-HP Wright engines roared to life one at a time: numbers one, two, three and four. This was her time to roar and no one argued with her. We could resume chatter in our mikes, once airborne. *Belle* groaned ever so slightly as she lifted off the runway. She flew to her spot in formation over the North Sea like a bird of prey in a flock with the rest of the 17s and transformed herself into a demon over German skies, lashing out at enemy fighters. Never once did I hear her utter a single complaint, though she did scream when flak ripped through her sides. Never once did she perform any way but flawlessly.

Belle flew through skies full of flak, her payload falling towards her target. *Belle* watched it drop, her destruction of Nazi Germany. On the way home, her nose seemed to turn slightly as she looked down surveying the damage that was done.

Every dragon has a chink in its armor. For *Belle*, it was her belly. Flak came from below, as did enemy fighters. They fired at the *Belle's* underside. With hundreds of holes shot through her, she flew on. With electrical systems down and hydraulics out she still flew on. *Belle* didn't need petrol to fly; we only gave it to her only because it was regulations. She didn't even need fumes in her tanks. *Belle's* wings could glide us back to Bassingbourn. There was nothing the Germans could do to stop her.

I sat with her on the runway, injured, when we returned from our mission in Bremen. I talked to her and comforted her. No matter how many holes the Nazis had shot through the *Belle*, I refused to let her die. I patched her damaged skin. I rewired her circuitry and put her nerves together again. I mended the hydraulics that pumped the blood through her veins.

Belle was my friend and I was hers. I rotated in the belly turret and protected her with my two .50-caliber Browning machine guns and thousands of rounds of ammunition. *Belle* and I will fly on together. "I will destroy anything, and I will kill anyone, who tries to harm you," I promised the *Belle*.

7

Solingen - Leverkusen

IT WAS A COLD MORNING AND STILL DARK. MOST MORNINGS are cold in Southern England in December, especially at five AM, but on this, the first morning of the month, there was a dry biting feel to the air. The stars were still clearly visible in the passing night sky. There was no cloud cover, and that meant there would be no delay forming the 17s over the North Sea.

The airbase at Bassingbourn was immense. After leaving the mess hall we attended briefing, then visited the chaplain and made our way to the runway. The 17s were barely visible in the distance. We had drawn short straw in briefing again. Our chins dropped when the *Belle,* along with sixteen other ships, was assigned to be part of the diversionary group. Still worse, the *Belle* was assigned the lowest altitude in the vertical wedge. We were going to get the brunt of the fighter and artillery attack. Some of the flyers in the main formation felt they would have it easier with the diversionary group taking on the entire Luftwaffe.

"We'll drop our payload and be back to Bassingbourn by nightfall," Quinn said. The sky over Western Germany was forecast to be clear and sunny. Unfortunately it was also forecast by our intelligence officers to be dark with flak and full of German fighters.

"You get any letters from home, Ras?" Charlie asked as we approached the *Belle*.

"Not this week, but I'm expecting something special for Christmas. I managed to get some cards off to the folks back home."

Belle was going through her final checklist. Incendiary bombs loaded and secured. Edelstein eyed what he considered his bombs. "That cutlery factory at Solingen is gonna be a thing of the past after today," he commented aloud and seemingly to himself. All the Browning machine guns were locked and loaded and ready to be tested on ascent. Parachutes were stowed in the fuselage.

The escape packs were strapped on our legs. I popped mine open for a long, reflective stare. Today's was a rough assignment. The 8th Air Force equipped us reasonably well in case we were shot down; equipped for an attempt at survival and escape, that is. In our escape pack was our picture in case we found our way to the resistance. The resistance made passports and thereby made it easier for us to travel across borders and get back to England. There were maps of the territories that we were bombing and a compass to find our way out. There was currency from different countries. There also were Benzedrine tablets, medicine that wired you up and allowed you to run faster and go long hours without sleep.

"This mission will be a maximum effort," the colonel had announced at the morning's briefing. Our crew had Solingen as its primary target and Leverkusen as the secondary target. At the eleventh hour Cecil Comer was assigned to fill in for John Hinda, the right waist gunner, who had frostbite. Cecil was on his first, and only flight with our crew.

The Wright engines came to life with a roar that filled the air. At first the number four engine turned slowly. I glanced a look of concern out of Charlie's gunner window toward the number four engine. Was the *Belle* trying to tell us something? Quinn's final checklist was complete and it was our turn down the runway. Our chatter stopped and we went to radio silence. The *Belle* cried like an angry tiger, eager to be unleashed.

In the Ruhr region in west central Germany, near the convergence of the Ruhr and Rhine Rivers, is a vast complex of industrial cities: Dussseldorf, Oberhausen, Cologne and many others. These industrial cities became one of the prime targets of the Allied bombing campaign. Sixty percent of Germany's steel and high-grade alloyed metals for weapons and aircraft engines were produced in this region. The Rhine River runs north south throughout this region and would serve as the last natural German defense to stop advancing American and British ground troops. The Rhine River also served as a landmark for American air sorties. In the Rhineland sits the steel city of Solingen, population of around 100,000, and Leverkusen, population of around 50,000, two industrial centers in the Ruhr region. Both cities are forty miles inside Germany's western border with the Netherlands, just east of the Rhine River, southeast of Dusseldorf and north of Cologne and Bonn. Both cities were heavily fortified with rings of antiaircraft banks circling them. German Messerschmitts protected both cities.

"Expect to run into heavy fighter attacks," the colonel had said at briefing.

Solingen was home to a major cutlery factory, making steak knives in peacetime but converted to make bayonets in wartime, bayonets that would kill American GIs on the beaches of Normandy seven months later. Our assignment was to destroy that factory; the secondary target was an industrial complex at Leverkusen. Some thirty P-47 Thunderbolts, assigned to the main formation, broke off fighter escort east of the Frisian Islands.

As we passed the Frisian Islands the main formation headed southeast. The diversionary group, with the *Belle* at the bottom, turned south towards the Rhineland flying at 27,000 feet and nearly 300 MPH. Nearing Solingen we dropped to 10,000 feet, bombing altitude, and slowed to 155 MPH, bombing speed, our most vulnerable time of the entire mission.

"Quinn, this flak's worse than a thunderstorm!" I shouted into my mike. The sky was raining flak. The shrapnel was so thick the *Belle* shook as the sky first turned black then white from the smoky trail of the antiaircraft fire. Dozens of flak shells tore holes through the *Belle's* fuselage. When the flak paused, a 20mm cannon burst from a Me-109 hit the *Belle*. It blew a hole a foot across the fuselage then ripped out the number one engine. A number of ships in our diversionary formation went down before reaching Solingen. But we reached our target and prepared to drop our payload. Edelstein lined up the factory in the Norden bombsite.

"We're there Quinn. Hold her steady," he said to himself. Edelstein unloaded the 8,000-pound payload, an early Christmas present from the *Belle* to Hitler, then turned control of the *Belle* back to Quinn.

I surveyed our remaining formation. "There's only six of us left, Quinn," I said in my mike. Surprisingly, my voice wasn't shaking. "Eleven ships have gone down." The pickings for Goering's boys from the diversionary group were getting thinner.

There was no need for the secondary target today; all the bombers that had made it to Solingen had managed to drop their payload on the cutlery factory. The *Belle* nosed up, falling behind the formation because she was unable to reach maximum cruising speed on three engines. She was still able to ascend at nearly three hundred feet per minute and methodically climbed, and turned southwest towards Belgium and run for home.

In the jungle, when animals run with the herd, they are safe. When they become separated from the herd, they are game for the hyenas. So too it was in the sky over Solingen. The formation provided a certain amount of protection against the German fighters but once a 17 fell behind, or the formation no longer existed, it was certain doom. Alone, the *Belle* would still be very dangerous for the Germans to bring down with eleven .50-caliber machine guns, two on top, two behind, one on each waist, two in the belly and one each for the radioman, bombardier and navigator. Quinn listed the *Belle* to one side or the other to allow the maximum number of 50s to focus on the incoming fighters.

The sky southwest of Solingen was infested with German Messerschmitt and Focke Wulf-190 fighters. I was doing the

"Messerschmitt twist" in the ball turret. It was a maneuver that command advised us to do whenever German fighters were around. By continuously rotating the turret, the fighter pilots knew that you were awake and on the lookout for them. Ideally we needed to ration our ammo, fight our way back to the coast, and pick up fighter escort over the North Sea. "Don't hold back now Charlie," I yelled into my mike. "There's no point in rationing our ammo today." By now every machine gun on the *Belle* was blazing.

An article that my father collected and showed to me after the war pertaining to this particular flight read, "American Flying Fortresses and Liberators in their third raid on Germany in three days, fought their way through clouds of Nazi fighters and bombed the Rhineland steel city of Solingen, southeast of Dusseldorf. Twenty-seven of the four-engine bombers were lost." I told my Dad after the war that fifteen of the seventeen ships in the diversionary group were shot down, one of those being the *Belle*.

"Two 109s, eleven o'clock level. They're coming in off the port side, Ras, out of the sun and closing fast. Range, two miles!" Dyer shouted into the intercom mike.

The first thing you see is the glare off the fighter's nose as it reflects the sun. "I see 'em Charlie. Concentrate on the forward one. I'll take the one nearest our bow."

"There's three more coming out from the cloud cover," Wingate, our top turret gunner said. "Seven o'clock low. Comer help me out!"

The first two Me-109s that closed in went down. The next hit our number two engine with a cannon burst. The engine was blown out with a force so hard that control of the ship was momentarily lost and the *Belle* turned completely over in mid-flight. Gas flow to the number two engine stopped and the propeller feathered. Now engines one and two were both out. Quinn righted the ship running on engines three and four only. The Me-109s closed in for the kill.

Comer, they're back on us from the starboard side," Wingate yelled. "We can't take one more hit."

German fighters nailed the number three engine with a volley of machine gun fire starting it on fire. Quinn was able to extinguish the fire by releasing CO2 from cylinders. The number three engine was the only engine on a B-17 with a generator. That turned the grim situation hopeless; a B-17 had one hundred nineteen electrical motors driving operations. Immediately the electrical motors stopped operating. Communication with our other ships was lost. Without electrical power, my ball turret locked in its position. The mikes went silent.

The *Belle* was at 27,000 feet and we were in trouble.

Some power is a lot better than no power when you're falling from five miles high. Three of the 1200 HP Wright engines were dead. The other one was probably dying. Air was screaming through the fuselage through the waist gunner's hatches. It screamed louder through the holes ripped through the *Belle*'s sides from cannon bursts and machine gun fire. The temperature was minus fifty degrees Fahrenheit. The electrically heated gloves stopped functioning. The power to the heated gloves ran in series, so when the generator went out, everyone's gloves lost heat. In order to bail out, time was of the essence. If we weren't attacked again on the way down, then we'd have the time but we had only a matter of minutes to complete our task.

I had to move fast, get out of the turret, into the main fuselage, put on my parachute, bail. The turret was too small to allow a chest pack parachute to be worn. I needed more time to get one on after getting into the fuselage. We always had confidence that in such a situation Quinn could hold the ship for as long as it took us to bail out. I knew the other crewmembers had to be harnessing their parachutes and bailing soon. We had been warned in briefing not to jump at too high an altitude as German fighters were shooting flyers as they floated down.

Time was running out. For me it was worse, much worse. There was only one way to escape the turret and when electrical power went out the turret froze, locked out of the "balled position" that allowed me to escape. The egress position from the turret where the gunner can escape into the fuselage was closed.

The *Belle* listed forward and began her descent.

Claustrophobia creates a special devil's brew. The space surrounding you closes in. You become short of breath. You are all alone. No one can come to your rescue and fear overwhelms you, an unrealistic fear, one that goes beyond being alone and in a closed space. It is a fear that replaces reality and robs you of rational thinking that can save your life. All that surrounds you closes in.

You hyperventilate, feeling suffocation even if there is plenty of oxygen. It's the reason I never went in tunnels with my brother Harry when I was a kid. I couldn't take being in a closed space. I just knew the dirt would cave in on me and I would suffocate. It would be a slow death, for there would be a pocket of air for me to suck on in my panicked state. I read stories when I was a kid about people who explored tunnels. Sometimes they became wedged and couldn't back up. Sometimes they would come to a stream and had to swim underneath the water hoping to come out in an air pocket. Sometimes they didn't find a pocket.

I had seen other 17s go down and knowing that the *Belle* was on her way down while I was trapped in the turret started a cascade toward claustrophobia. I knew the outcome. Crippled ships landed with the turret gunner trapped inside. He was crushed to death or maybe burned on a suicide mission. I was all alone, trapped inside a Plexiglas ball. Vibrations from the machine guns had stopped. If anyone was alive, they must have jettisoned and I hadn't seen their chutes.

The Sperry ball turret was only four feet in diameter. On a normal mission the ball turret gunner sits, back to the ball, holding onto the handgrips that operate the turret and the machine guns. The gun sight is positioned in front of his chest. The machinery to operate turret and everything inside it are all electrically powered. All of them froze up when the number three engine was demolished by machine gun fire. It was as if the Germans had reached out and put a metal rod into the rotating gears, creating a trap for the belly turret gunner to die in when his 17 crashed and burned. My porthole was six inches in diameter and oil was streaking across it creating an illusion of an even smaller compartment.

The *Belle* tipped steeper.

The turret has a backup device similar to a Victrola crank. It allows the turret to be manually cranked by hand until it lines itself back into the ball position with the guns pointing straight back. That allows a rear door to be opened as an escape hatch into the fuselage. The crank on the upper right side of the turret was used to rotate the ball and on the upper left, to change the elevation. Both were mounted in clips and held in place with safety wire. The cramped space of the turret did not allow me to turn around to get at them. I was wedged.

The scream of the air racing through the ship got louder as the roar of the Wright engines lessened and *Belle's* nose listed down. I glanced out between the streaks of oil on the porthole. I had counted parachutes when 17s went down wondering if the crew was able to bail from their stricken craft. Rarely did I ever see ten. Now I had another answer: the belly turret gunner was caught in the Plexiglas trap and couldn't bail out. So far, still no chutes from our crew. Maybe Quinn was trying to buy more time for our crew to get out. The sweat that formed on my forehead instantly froze.

The *Belle* was falling.

The turret was closing in around me. The handgrips had grown to fill the entire space inside the turret. When the oxygen mask worked, it worked in a demand mode. Sucking on it delivered the oxygen. There was no oxygen left in the lines. At high altitudes with no oxygen you can do crazy things and don't even know it. I stepped on the foot pedal to operate my mike. "Shoot me Charlie!" I yelled. "Shoot me." I thought it would be a better option than the impending crash. "I'm not going to die like this." But the mike wasn't functioning either.

I had to get out of the turret and at the rate the *Belle* was falling there wasn't enough time. I ripped off the inoperative electrically heated gloves; underneath was a fine pair of recently issued silk gloves that kept my skin from adhering to the cold medal parts of the turret. I had the slightest smile as my mind drifted back to graduation from Laredo Arial Gunnery School. With the help of some quickly said prayers I broke the cranks' safety wires. Using the small cranks, I started rotating the crankshaft that moved the turret into the neutral escape position. It moved so slowly that you couldn't even tell if the turret was rotating. It took dozens of turns of the shaft, then, only inch-by-inch seemed to rotate the turret.

The *Belle's* number four engine still had power.

I could start to make out the tops of trees racing towards me. A thought raced through my mind. Maybe Quinn was using the one remaining engine to flatten out the steep descent just before we crashed landed. The escape hatch lined up. Charlie and Cecil were over my turret helping to line it up for me.

"Move your ass," Charlie yelled as he shoved the turret door open behind me.

"Did the others bail?" I shouted over the screaming air.

"No. The crew is all on board. Quinn thinks our best option is to crash land. He's gliding the ship down trying to buy you time to get out of there."

On this fateful December 1, 1943 none of our crew bailed out. Quinn had made the decision to crash the *Belle* and not bail. His decision is what gave me the borrowed time that I needed to work my way out of the turret. He had saved my life.

The *Belle* and ground were but a moment from each other.

Move! We were coming down at an angle that increased body pressure. Movement was not easy, barely possible. Charlie, Cecil and I crawled our way to the cramped space of the radio room where we joined Steiler and McDowell. We braced ourselves, backs to the empty fuselage, facing forward and hanging on for our lives. Steiler, our radio operator, had cast out many of the removable objects from the area to prevent the danger of them flying about and killing us on impact. This included five of the six radio packs, the radio operator's flexible machine gun, and a chair. Meanwhile, up front, Hornbeck the navigator, Falleck our co-pilot and Quinn were completing their tasks with a series of adjustments.

The *Belle* was going to crash.

To my last day I thanked our crew, especially Quinn, for his ability to bring the *Belle* in, the Good Lord for watching over us as we crashed on German soil, in all locations, a plowed field. I thanked the *Belle* for holding together. I watched the sky out of the gun position at the top of the radio room; seconds later I saw the ground through the same opening; then the sky again. The *Belle* had done a complete rollover before touching down a second time. The contact sheered off the landing gear. It took a little over a half mile from impact before we ran into a pile of rutabagas and came to a complete stop.

The *Belle* was dead and in an open field near the Belgium border. We were all alive.

8

Capture

WE WERE JUST SOUTH OF DUREN IN WESTERN GERMANY. Up front, Hornbeck had a bad concussion and wasn't making any sense. Falleck and Edelstein were shaken up but otherwise all right. All of us in the radio room felt as if we had just ridden in a bronco-busting contest at the county fair. Steiler's face was frozen white from frostbite. I had a terrific pain in the left side of my chest from an empty ammunition box that had hit me during the first impact of our crash. Except for that, none of us were the worse for it.

"Bert should have pitched the empty ammo cans," I mumbled.

McDowell, Charlie, and I left the *Belle* to discover that she had bounced over two stone hedgerows. "Will you look at that Charlie?" I asked. "The ship just missed those hedgerows. It could have come apart at the seams or turned into a fireball. Instead it runs into a pile of rutabagas!"

Charlie was studying my reactions. "You okay, Ras?"

"Yeah. I'm okay."

"Looked like you'd seen a ghost when we pulled you out of the turret."

"I'm fine."

"Boy, this is something," Comer said, getting out of the *Belle*. "I get assigned one time to this ship and we crash land!"

"Let's torch her ASAP." McDowell said staring at the *Belle*.

Training included destruction of our plane to prevent the Germans from learning engineering secrets, including the engines, armament, and the turret's operation among other things. There on German soil sat the *Belle*, still intact. Unknown to us, the Germans already had a number of undamaged B-17s that had been shot down. Charlie went back to the *Belle* to get one of the sixty-four pound waist guns.

"Shoot the *Belle* with the flares," Falleck ordered. We did, but the *Belle* refused to burn.

By this time the first local people arrived at the scene, two Polish prisoners who had been working in a nearby field. They were very excited, hoping that the Americans had arrived to liberate them. Their excitement turned to despair after realizing what had actually happened.

"Now what?" Comer asked.

"We make a stand here," answered McDowell. "There're still our waist guns and the top turret."

"What are we going to use for ammo, Mac?" I asked. "I'm down to two remaining cans. Besides, you can't defend a position like this. It will give the German home guard a perfect excuse to kill all of us. They'll call for a tank and blow the ship apart. Bert threw out our only hand held machine gun about ten miles back. What did you do that for anyway, Bert?" I was starting to cough up blood. My breathing was okay so I figured it wasn't a punctured lung; maybe just bruised from being hit by the ammo box.

"They told us at briefing that the Krauts are much more likely to shoot us if we're armed," Bert answered. "That's why they stopped issuing handguns in the first place. I just thought it would be better get rid of that gun too."

You believed them?" I was a little testy. We stood there for a moment looking at our injured and getting more anxious.

"Well, we're not going to get away carrying Hornbeck on our backs," Charlie said.

And you're not going very far carrying that Browning, Charlie."

"What are we going to do, Ras?" Falleck asked. He had tears running down his cheeks. Falleck was a good soldier, but I couldn't resist a little dig.

"You're the officer," I said. "You tell us."

"But you're older." The guys had started calling me "Pop" since I turned twenty-three the previous August.

The rest of the crew went silent. I was looking at the map from my escape kit. "They'll be looking for us to the west of here. We split up like, make our way to Belgium and contact the resistance." Our counter-intelligence had told us at morning briefing to get away from any downed craft as soon as possible and hide. The theory for hiding was that the Germans would search out our plane and surrounding areas for the crew, and at some point, leave the area and look elsewhere.

I picked out some points on the map. "Comer, Steiler and McDowell head south toward Euskirchen. Edelstein, you and Charlie head south toward Zuipich. Falleck, you come with me. We'll head north toward Duren. The first chance you guys get to use your currency, buy whatever provisions are available." Each of us had about four hundred dollars in assorted currency. "Make sure you use the German money to pay for things. Right now, it's best to get as far away from here as possible, lay low for a night or two, then blend in as best as you can. Try to get at least ten miles from the *Belle* before nightfall. After the Krauts have stopped searching around here, then try to go west to Belgium and make your way back home." The odds that any of us would make it back home were remote but it was a goal all downed flyers aimed for.

Before leaving, I walked back over to Quinn and Wingate. They were trying to start the *Belle* on fire. "Get outta here," Quinn said.

"I owe you, Quinn." I turned and walked back to where the rest of the crew was making last minute preparations to leave. "Let's go, Falleck, I said. "Bert, if you get your hands on another machine gun don't throw it away." The seven of us were off on a dead run towards a nearby forest.

Once there we split up and headed towards three different points of the compass.

We didn't know it at the time, but the first German civilian on the scene was Johan Richter. Then other curious persons came running to see the downed plane. Richter, as it turned out, had seen the plane crash near his small village of Drove near Duren. He was an avid photographer since youth. He later became a German Architect. In 1973 Richter wrote a report for a 91st Memorial Society paper, "The Ragged Irregular." How Richter came across the Memorial Society paper is an interesting story in itself. Woodrow B. Hood II of Long Beach, California, the son of a career Air Force father, in turn joined the Air Force himself as soon as he was old enough in 1966. During his service he married a German girl who turned out to be Richter's daughter. While looking through his father-in-law's photo album, he found pictures of the downed American plane. Study indicated it was a 91st aircraft and he contacted the "Ragged Irregular," which was able to positively identify it as one belonging to the 401st Squadron. Edward E. Pinkowski was the original crew chief and Matt Peters was assistant crew chief. Lt. John Quinn was then assigned pilot. Hood told Richter about the Memorial Society and his story was told in the "Ragged Irregular." The report was entitled "Down in Germany-Eye Witness Report." The report focused on when an American B-17 landed in Germany after a bombing raid. How did the German civilian populace react? How did they feel? What did they do? An eyewitness account by a German, Richter, who not only saw the 91st plane *Hell's Belle* LLG 23060 come down, but took pictures at the scene. The pictures give the impression of curiosity, and to some degree sympathy for Quinn, Hornbeck and Wingate. Here's Richter's story as told in 1973: "I first saw the flight of a Fortresses flying at a very high altitude over my little village of Drove about 10:00 AM going in a southeasterly direction. In about two hours the planes came back, this time flying much lower. One of them was flying very low with both engines on the left stopped and the propellers not rotating. A few miles further on the plane made a crash landing in a farm field. It was a very skillful landing, uphill on a small hill, just beside a little valley. As the plane was making its long landing descent it passed within 300 yards of German troops training in a nearby woods. The landing gear was knocked off when they struck a huge pile of turnips."

Meanwhile, a German soldier on leave from the Russian front arrived at the scene and put Quinn, Wingate, and Hornbeck under arrest. He was part of the home guard. They were taken to the Bugermeister's (mayor) house in nearby Boich. The Bugermeister, Karl Norden, was very much an anti-Nazi. He and his wife fed the captured crewmen. The village's only interpreter, a priest, tried to assure them that they would be well treated. He also told them that there were no SS men in the area and they had nothing to fear. Later that same day, two "civilians" came by and took all three away. Quinn and Hornbeck ended up in the officer's Stalag. Wingate was on his way to Stalag 17B.

Falleck and I headed north on a dead run. Within the hour both of us had taken the Benzedrine tablets from our escape kits and were running three feet off the ground. During the next few hours we managed to out-run, out-hide and out-distance several small groups from the home guard who were in hot pursuit. The first night Falleck and I spent in a culvert unable to sleep. We didn't have an appetite thanks to the Benzedrine tablets.

"Let's go over the plan to get back to England again," Falleck said as we were hiding in the culvert.

"We find our way through Belgium to France," I said. "Then meet up with the 'Free French' who smuggle us down to the southern border and put us in contact with a Spanish mountain guide. He's going to get us over the Pyrenees and into Spain, 'for an agreed fee,' which we bargain for and promise him that our government will pay once our trusting guide delivers us to our embassy."

By the end of the second day, Falleck and I were just northwest of Duren, some twenty-five miles from the crash site. We walked through woods the Germans had cleaned and in America would look like a park, down roads with normal traffic and no one paid any attention. In busy areas we didn't stand out. We even had to cross a bridge with German guards on one end. A light snow was falling covering the top of our flight jackets.

"Get rid of our hats and just use some hand motions. Don't say anything out loud," I told Falleck. The German guards on the bridge weren't even curious about us. The second night we found shelter in an old shed that we vacated before dawn the next morning.

Our escape ended at a forbidden zone, "verboten" the sign read. The Germans crisscrossed their entire nation with forbidden zones. Only the locals knew the times not to trespass in these areas. Interned workers, downed airmen and all others in the given area at a given time of the day were shot without warning if they tried to cross. In this case, the zone was a thirty-acre open field. After jumping over a small knoll Falleck and I leaned back to take a rest. Little did we know that the knoll was actually a gun emplacement manned by the three members of the home guard. I felt a gun at the back of my head. The fellow at the other end was an older man, about fifty, who was shaking so hard I thought his shaking was going to discharge his rifle.

"What are we going to do?" Falleck asked.

"There's nothing we can do, Falleck, and don't do anything stupid or they'll shoot us."

The Germans were shouting commands and motioning to the back of a truck. Then, they transported us back to where the *Belle* had gone down. That's the way the Germans did it, I suppose, in order to make a record of how many of a given crew had been captured. It was then on by truck to Boich, the same little hamlet where Quinn, Hornbeck, and Wingate had been turned over to the civilian authority two days earlier. On arrival we were ordered out of the truck and marched through the main street of the hamlet. The local people, who had obviously been informed of our capture, lined the street.

"Fliegergangster," they shouted, as they threw sticks, stones and dirt and spit at us.

"They've convinced me we're not welcome here, Falleck," I said. "I don't think they have any love in their hearts for the two of us." As we marched into the mayor's yard, we sighted a wagon conveniently pushed back under a barn rafter with two ropes in place. The ropes were not just for display. They had no doubt been used before. It looked like there was to be a public hanging of two newly captured U.S. Airmen.

"Falleck," I said, "These people are not about to hang me. It will be far better taking our chances on getting shot trying to outrun the guards."

I had no more finished my thought with Falleck when one of our guards who, unknown to us understood and spoke English, said, "I wouldn't try escaping. Besides, Bugermeister Norden has different plans for you."

We were marched into the mayor's house. He seemed to be an understanding fellow and even a bit sympathetic. His wife appeared in a side doorway, crying. The priest was in the room and told us in unbroken English about their son. "The mayor and his wife have a son in the German Army. He has been captured and taken prisoner and is in an American POW camp in Brownsville, Texas. She is uncertain about his fate."

I quickly seized the opportunity. "I was assigned guard duty at Brownsville before gunnery school," making up a story as fast as my thoughts could organize something that made sense. "I can assure you that the captured soldiers are treated in accordance with the Geneva Convention. They are well cared for in America." Frau Norden left the room, returning momentarily from the kitchen with cookies for Falleck and me.

The phone rang. The mayor spoke enough words for us to be certain who was the focus of the conversation. Time seemed to stop, as did the conversation. The mayor, his wife, and priest left the room. Falleck and I were left alone in the room with guards at the door. Two hours later, German soldiers arrived to pick us up. We were transported to a Federal prison in Duren. It was December 3, 1943.

Back home, some ten days after we had been shot down, my dad received a Western Union telegram from the Secretary of War notifying my family that I was reported missing in action over Germany and expressing his regret. There was no report whether or not the crew of the *Hell's Belle* was alive or dead. Dad, usually a stoic man not inclined to swear, swore a blue streak that day about the Germans.

"You better go to school and show this to your Mom," he said giving the telegram to my sisters, Evelyn and Phyllis.

They rushed down to the one-room school where Mom taught kindergarten through eighth grade to twelve students. Among other duties, Mom was getting ready for the annual Christmas program.

"We got a notice about Bill," Evelyn exclaimed, handing the telegram to Mom who promptly collapsed. It wasn't until a month later that my family received news that I was still alive.

9

Federal Prison to Dulag Luft

IT WAS LATE IN THE AFTERNOON, ON DECEMBER 4, 1943, WHEN the truck pulled up to the prison dock. It was the last time I saw Falleck. From the Bugermeister's house we were transported under armed guard by truck to the Federal prison at Duren. There, the SS tortured and killed prisoners. The guards forced us to watch the merciless killing of interned French and Yugoslavian workers. At any given time of the day or night screams filled the air, then shots were heard. You could only imagine whom the shots were for and who was next.

The guards took my jacket, boots and stockings. I was placed in a cell on the second floor measuring five feet wide by seven feet long with a high ceiling and a window eight feet off the floor that measured eight by twelve inches. The room had a cement floor. It was cold and damp and had a musty odor, the kind you smell when you go down to the cellar to get some pickled cucumbers or old potatoes in the winter months. My bunk was a wooden shelf that was hinged to the wall. In the middle of the cell was a small table with a jar of water and a jar of dark tea.

Twenty minutes passed when the cell door swung open and a German guard ordered me to follow him. This clipped winged flyer did so without argument.

"Look here, bud," I demanded of the guard. "Someone's got my flyer's jacket and boots. I'd like 'em back." I didn't know it then but I wasn't going to see that warm, fleece-lined, flyer's jacket ever again. I later figured if the German Army needed our clothes, then they didn't have enough gear for their own army. I continued barefooted down a wooden stairway to a first floor room where a Canadian Flight Sergeant was resting in a chair. He had an injured left leg.

"You will change his dressing," the guard ordered with a smirk on his face. "There are supplies on the counter. You are verboten to talk to each other," he said. I felt proud to help the Canadian.

On the counter was a bottle of saline, clean gauze to wrap the wound and a pair of old scissors. The Canadian soldier's face was red, as if he had a fever. On closer inspection it was evident that his foot was missing. His pants had been shredded. I could only imagine how he had lost his leg. He was dirty and must have been in the prison for some time. As I unwrapped the dressing I thought of an old adage my father use to tell his boys when we started to complain how bad we had it about one thing or another: "I complained about having no shoes until I met a man who had no feet."

Upon removing the wet dressing a putrid smell came from the wound. It was obvious why the German medics had asked an American POW to do their work: the stump was grossly infected. Red streaks ran up the Canadian's leg. He had cellulites. I bit on my back teeth and took in a sudden slight gasp. The Canadian soldier looked like he was about to cry. Certainly he was thinking about the foot he had lost and the leg he might lose.

"It's alright," I told him, nodding my head, trying to get a better grip on the situation.

"Got any ether?" I asked the guard. Dad kept ether at his pharmacy and I knew ether would kill just about anything. The guard wasn't talking.

With some clean gauze, wetted with the saline, I wiped the pus from the stump as best I could. The more I wiped, the more the wound bled. I finished dressing the wound by applying dry gauze to the stump, and then I was escorted back to my cell.

A half-hour later a bowl of potato soup was pushed under my door. Surprisingly the aroma of the soup filled the little cell the minute the guard left. I took one spoonful. It tasted good but I was still thinking about that Canadian soldier and wasn't hungry enough to eat anything. A short time later, when the guard returned for my dish, he informed me in his broken English, "You will learn to eat." I was in solitary confinement in that cell for seven days and never received another bit of food of any kind, only dark tea. I began to feel weak after a few days. Never again while I was in prison did I refuse food.

On the eighth day of captivity—December 12, 1943—groups of POWs were transported by truck to an airport at Cologne about fifteen miles north of Duren and locked in a room in one of the smaller buildings. It was just few miles from our secondary target at Leverkusen. It was here that I first experienced Allied raids.

Look, there're B-17s in bombing formation!" shouted a POW while he pointed out a window.

"We need to find a protected area," another POW yelled.

"Jump into a window depression," the first answered. Every place that afforded protection from the concussion was quickly occupied. There we crouched with our knees close to our chests and our ears covered to dampen the sound. High demolition bombs fell shaking the ground and leveling buildings. The sound was terrifying.

"Man, I'm glad they're gone," another one of the prisoners said. "I wonder if the Krauts let the Allies know they're keeping American POWs on the airbase?" If they did, it didn't slow down the bombing.

"It looks like a giant Christmas tree," another of the POWs said later that night. It was the flares dropping ahead of the British bombers that continued the pounding at night. By dawn, the airfield and most of the surrounding buildings were destroyed.

For the next two days we were made to dig bodies out of the debris caused by allied bombing after which we were herded onto the open back of a German army truck and taken to Frankfurt on the Main. The men sat silently in the back of the truck, forbidden by the German guards to talk. It was a clear and cold winter's day. None of the Americans wore jackets.

No Allied bombers appeared, so it was uneventful during our travel to Frankfurt. It took most of the day to travel southeast through Bonn and down to the Main. Destruction was all around. On one hand, it seemed inevitable that the Germans could not withstand the pounding from the constant bombing, and on the other hand, it seemed inevitable that they would take their vengeance out on us. As we traveled through the center of Frankfurt you could see that one city block after another had been leveled. The guards stared at us. In Frankfurt we were corralled with other POWs.

"Hey Ras!" It was Charlie! Steiler, Comer, Wingate and McDowell were with him!

"Hey, you guys," I was smiling from ear to ear. What a reunion it was knowing they were still alive.

"What happened to you, Bert?" I asked. Steiler was nursing open sores across his nose and on his cheeks.

"It's the frostbite I got the day the *Belle* was shot down. That's why Mac and I had to turn ourselves in. I needed medical attention."

We rehashed the last ten days until the afternoon when we were marched two blocks away to an interrogation center, "Dulag Luft." There the Germans isolated the POWs as best they could. My assignment was, once again, to a solitary cell with a shelf for a bed, only this time my cell did not have a window making it worse than the cell at the Federal prison. There you could at least tell night from day. It was a smaller cell with a heavy wooden door that blocked any contact with the rest of the prison. The guards controlled its heating unit.

"If you require anything, then you must trip the metal lever at the left of the door," the guard instructed. The lever notified the guard that a visit to the "sand-box" was necessary. You were allowed to make a request for a drink of water in the same way. The guards were always slow to respond.

Alone in my cell, I heard a tapping on one wall. Either the prisoner in the next cell was trying to practice the Morse code or he was a radio operator trying to make conversation. In any case, I never knew just what he had to say because I was taken to see the interrogation officer. Two huge SS guards stood outside his office on either side of his door.

There I met Major Rolfing. Cigarette smoke permeated his large office. The only chair was behind his cluttered desk along with a picture of the Fuehrer. Rolfing's mannerisms suggested that he was full of himself. He was a decorated veteran, with a lot of medals decorating his uniform. He looked to be between fifty-five and sixty years old, five feet nine inches tall and had a slight potbelly. I stood at attention and waited while Rolfing paced the floor, checking me out.

As he walked toward me with his ice-cold stare, I thought about this individual and everything the Germans represented. "Cigarette, Sergeant?" It was his first and only congenial gesture. I took a handful. I didn't smoke but cigarettes were good trading items. "What are your name, rank and serial number?" Rolfing said in his German accent.

"William E. Rasmussen, Staff Sergeant, United States Air Force, B16064955."

"What are the names of your other crew members? Where is your plane depot located and what air-wing do you fly with?"

"William E. Rasmussen, Staff Sergeant, United States Air Force, B16064955."

My answer didn't seem to score any points with Rolfing. "What got you all those medals?" I asked him. The Major ignored my question.

"You may go, Herr Rasmussen. I have no further use for you."

Guards escorted me back to solitary confinement, but thirty minutes later I had my second trip to Rolfing's office. He no longer carried a friendly manner. It might be part of his act but not being absolutely sure, I stood there at attention, tired, barefooted, smelling badly. I may have looked much less the American soldier without my boots and without flyer's jacket but felt every bit his equal.

"Herr Rasmussen, what are the names of you crew members? What air-wing do you fly with? Where is your plane depot?"

"Were you given one of those medals for interrogating American flyers?" I asked.

"Just answer the question!" he shouted, spitting in my face.

"William E. Rasmussen, Staff Sergeant United States Army Air Force, B16064955."

Rolfing's faced reddened

"Take him back to his cell."

I passed the time unable sleep lying on the wooden shelf. A few hours went by before, once again, it was back to my interrogator. The results were similar, but the Major was getting more impatient with my lack of cooperation. Each time he questioned me, I asked him another question about his medals. Rolfing always asked me where our plane depot was located but I couldn't provide an answer even if I wanted to, because I didn't know. As a matter of fact, it always amazed me when there were more aircraft to replace those that had been lost or damaged, although I didn't tell Rolfing that. If ten B-17s were lost or damaged, ten new 17s were on the runway the next morning. The only way to stop the replacement bombers would be to attack the factories in America, something the Germans were never able to do. If needed, one hundred new flyers replaced the lost flyers at morning's briefing. Rolfing wanted to know what wing we flew with, and that was something he should have been able to figure out without my help. The letter "A" was painted on our tail assembly and any interrogation officer should have known that the *Belle* was a ship in the 1st Wing, but I refused to answer. Once again, it was back to my cell.

Life in solitary left a lot to be desired, staring at four blank walls hours on end. Not knowing what was coming next kept my mind racing in circles. The guards worked hard at making it as uncomfortable as possible. They would turn the up heat until it was extremely hot in your cell, then turn it off so you would freeze.

"It's not going to bother me to be cold," I told myself, letting my mind wander. "I know how to deal with the cold." Growing up in northern

Michigan had taught me that. My mom always got after me when I was a kid because I didn't wear boots, or gloves, or a hat with ear warmers even when there was a blizzard. I shivered, but refused to admit that I was cold.

I thought about home. My parents owned the drug store in Cedar. Harry and I used to stock the soda cooler with ice from our icehouse. We made ice picks by cutting a piece of an old broom handle, about a foot long, then pounding a nail into one end of the handle. All that was left to do was cut the flat head of the nail off. The ice picks made it easy to get the blocks separated from each other when they were needed for the soda cooler that was just inside the front entrance of the store. On hot summer days, it was the first thing that the customers saw when they entered the store. The block of ice sat in the middle of the metal cooler with ice water all around it. The cooler was stocked with orange and pineapple pop, Dad's Root Beer, RC Cola and 7-Up all in standup bottles. On the weekends, when we worked in the store, Mom would let us have a bottle of pop in the morning and one in the afternoons.

The icehouse was a small shed, just behind our house. It was under a large maple tree that shaded it in the summer. But in winter, Dad had Harry and I cut the blocks of ice from a frozen inland lake. We used a chisel-shaped blade that was welded onto the end of a six-foot metal rod and carved out the one-foot square blocks of ice. The trick was to get the ice out in one piece without busting through the ice into the freezing water, until you were almost done, or you'd get wet. When you got wet, you got cold, especially if the wind picked up. Sometimes I'd use an ax to chip open one spot, then a saw with large teeth to cut the block of ice free. Harry and I cut the blocks of ice from just two or three places in the lake because the hole would freeze solid again during the night. Fresh cut ice always looked nicer in the soda cooler because it was clear, without the trapped snow inside of it. The trapped snow made it impossible to see through it. Sometimes, we would stay out on the lake for an hour or two and fish for perch or bass.

Harry was ready with instructions whenever we were set to go, calling it a day only after it started to get dark. "Load the ice onto the sled so we can pull it back to the shed," he would say. Because he was older than I was, it meant that I had to load the two or three blocks onto the sled and pull it back to the icehouse. Harry supervised. In the corner of the icehouse were boxes of sawdust that were collected throughout the year. Sawdust was quite valuable since it made great insulation.

Paper made insulation too, but there wasn't any inside my cell, if there was I could roll up in it and stay warm. "Stack the sawdust a half an inch between blocks and an inch on top of the ice," Harry would bark. Over the winter, we filled the icehouse to the top, over eight feet high and ten feet square filled with blocks of ice, each insulated with the sawdust packing that prevented the ice from melting all summer long.

Usually, by the time we got done with our chore, we were wet and cold. We were shaking and our lips were blue but we didn't care. We were having fun. So, I laughed inside at the German guards who thought they were getting to me, and just thought about the winters back home.

Chow at Dulag Luft came in the form of a bowl of thin soup served once a day. Every few days it came with a piece of black bread, often with mold on it. I ate every bit of nourishment the Germans allowed, no matter how sparse and no matter how moldy. That guard at the Federal prison had been right. I did learn to eat everything that was served.

I made a conscious effort to keep track of the date. I wondered what it would be like to spend Christmas in one of these cells. It would be nice to be back in Cedar with my family. It was so pretty at home during the holiday season with fresh snow on the ground and the Christmas lights up. Everyone had to be shopping for presents to exchange on Christmas morning. Mom would have decorated the tree by now. Our family band would play Christmas music. Music was a big part of our family, filling our days as we grew up. Our family had its own orchestra for entertainment and it was a heck of a good one too. Mother played the piano, Dad played the sousaphone, my older sister

Evelyn played the clarinet and my younger sister Phyllis the organ. Harry and I both played the trumpet. I loved music, especially big band and Dixie. Our family band played on birthdays, on holidays and every Sunday afternoon. I enjoyed the Christmas holiday best of all. Our family opened presents in the mornings before going to church. Christmas dinner was always turkey with dressing, mashed potatoes with turkey gravy and candied yams. After dinner we played Christmas songs, like *O' Come All Ye Faithful* and, of course, *Silent Night*. There wasn't going to be any music in this place and certainly no Christmas meal.

The guards let me write a short letter home, although it didn't get there until March. Undoubtedly, German POWs were being allowed to write a letter home. The Germans had to allow American POWs the same privilege. The guards gave strict rules on what we could say. "All letters will be censored," a guard said. "You may say where you are being held, that you are in good health and are being treated according to the Geneva Convention. Your family must not write to you at Dulag Luft because this is not your final destination. Say nothing about what has happened to you or your crew since you have been taken prisoner or the letter will be thrown away."

It had been nineteen days since the *Belle* was shot down. Most of them I had spent in solitary confinement. Getting a glimpse out of a window when I was escorted to the john was the only way I could guess what time it was.

Six days after my last visit, a few pieces of black bread served with soup and I was back in Rolfing's office. It was in the evening of December 20, and just when I was trying to get some sleep. The Major was quite anxious, pacing back and forth like someone had rattled his cage. I stood at attention. Suddenly he stopped pacing.

"I am through with your stubbornness to cooperate," he shouted. "Sergeant, I am aware what your soldier's manual states. As a prisoner of war you are to tell the withholding powers, only your name, rank and serial number. You are aware of what it is that I require from you. This will be your final chance to cooperate. Nowhere does it state that you cannot write it down. Take this pencil and paper, return to your cell and complete the questions for me. Do you understand?"

"Yes sir," I answered.

I accepted the pencil and paper and returned to my cell thinking that my final hours were close at hand. If Rolfing thought, even for a moment, that he was going to get any help from me, he was sadly mistaken. I sat down on the shelf, looked at the blank paper for a few minutes then very slowly wrote, William E. Rasmussen, Staff Sergeant United States Air Force, B16064955. I folded the paper and waited.

In short order, the hob-nailed shoes of the escort service came down the hall. He opened the door and collected the folded note. In about ten minutes those same footsteps could be heard only with a faster cadence than the first time. "Rouse," he shouted and with pulling, tugging and lots of shoving rushed me back to Rolfing's office.

"You are of no use to me!" Rolfing yelled. His hand slipped under the edge of his desk to push a button. The SS troopers appeared through the door. "Get rid of him," the Major ordered, his finger pointing at me. The SS guards dragged me out of Rolfing's office down to the end of the building, one guard on each side, their arms wrapped under my armpits.

The complex was built like a spider's web. The solitary cells were placed in long tentacle-like rows. The body was the control station including Rolfing's office. By the time we reached the end of the row, my feet were only occasionally touching the floor. Once outside, I was thrown into the crawl space under the building. It was pitch black and couldn't have been over twenty degrees. Wearing only a shirt and slacks, I got very cold very quickly. The only redeeming feature was the cement foundation that blocked most of the wind that screamed as it tried to find its way between the foundation and the floorboards. I felt good about the fact that I hadn't helped Rolfing find the answers to his questions.

I sat there on the cold dirt, arms hugging my chest, trying to stay warm, wondering what the next few hours might bring. I tried not to think about the days or weeks ahead. It was impossible not to think about home. Every few seconds the wind let out a short, high-pitched shriek. It was the same noise the wind made back home when Harry and I filled the icehouse in the middle of winter. I didn't think much of it then. We were dressed for the cold weather. I did now.

Within a few minutes, someone or something was making its way through the dark in my direction. I thought it was part of the Rolfing's strategy to get me to talk. "Who are you?" I asked.

"John Winant, and you?"

"Bill Rasmussen, Sergeant, United States Air Force. What baseball team does Stan the Man play for?" I demanded an answer from Winant, not knowing what to expect, thinking he was a plant.

"St. Louis. What and where do the Giants and Bears play?" It was Winant's turn to ask me questions.

"Football, New York and Chicago," I answered.

"Glad to meet you, Sarg."

"Likewise, Winant. How long you been under here?"

"Just a few hours. I refused to make a propaganda speech on German radio that they want to beam to the English-speaking people across the continent. They're going to try again because I overheard them say that they're going to give me a shot of pentothal." He sounded nervous, but we talked. I found out that he was the son of the American ambassador to England

"It's kinda cold, think Jerry (our slang name for the Germans) forgot to turn the heat on?" I asked, still shivering and trying to make light of the situation. Winant was lost in thought.

"If you make it back before me," he said a moment later, "please notify our embassy that I was forced to make the speech by the Germans. I'm never going to do anything for them on my own free will. Tell my dad that I tried to be a good soldier and was thinking about him and Mom."

The more I talked to him, the more I thought he was a good soldier. It kind of surprised me because he was the son of the ambassador. Winant had thick skin and was strong-minded and was trying his best to avoid doing the German's bidding. What wasn't clear to me was why he assumed that I would make it home and he wouldn't, but we did make a pact.

"I'll call your parents and tell them the same about you if I get out and you don't," he promised. We sat and talked through the night. At daybreak the guards opened the small door to the crawl space and ordered us out.

"Don't forget our pact," he said when we were separated.

"I won't."

Sixty-seven captured American flyers were herded into the yard in front of Rolfing. "Now that the officers have finished a fine meal of corn beef and cabbage, I can take the time to inform you, with pride, that your case at Dulag Luft is closed. All of your crewmembers have been accounted for. They have either been captured or are confirmed dead. You will be transported to a prisoner of war camp." With that he turned and walked away.

10

Dulag Luft to Stalag 17B

THE WIND WASN'T BLOWING AND THERE WAS NO SNOW. BUT, the twenty-second day in December 1943 had been very cold. The ex-flyers, now prisoners of war, were heading southeast away from Frankfurt, toward Linz, then on to Krems, Austria. We had been inside a boxcar for ten hours, trying to keep warm as the transport train rumbled on.

Apart from the brief statement given by Major Rolfing at Dulag Luft, the POWs hadn't been told a thing. The enlisted men had been separated from the officers who were on their way to a prison camp in Barth, in northeast Germany. The prison guards had taken our uniforms and given us old uniforms from countries the Nazis had overrun. I got an old Serb uniform along with newly issued footwear, a pair of wooden clogs. Taking away the Air Force uniforms gave the Germans the added benefit of demeaning the American flyers. Without our uniform, we didn't look like American soldiers.

None of this meant anything. The only concern of the ex-flyers now was how to stay warm. The temperature had been in the low twenties in Frankfurt and dropped even lower when night took over. There was no heat provided for our journey. With the door shut and locked, the body heat of sixty-seven men in a small boxcar was all there was to provide warmth. It is impossible to relate how cold it is when you are thinly dressed and hour after hour goes by with no relief. The men in the boxcar became very cold and shivered continuously.

As I sat on the floor trying to fall asleep through the constant clickity-clack of the rolling train, my mind once again wondered back home. I remembered being eleven years old and asking my dad about going to Manistee so I could fly in an airplane, my dream for years. That was a special time. When I was a kid, the one thing that always got my attention, was any type of aircraft that flew across the sky. I left whatever I was doing to scan the heavens for the approaching airplane. Many a time, I wished that I had been born one of the Wright brothers, or Charles Lindbergh. The Traverse City Airport had a craft that flew every day, one hundred thirty miles, from Grand Rapids to Traverse City with its cargo of mail and the daily paper. "I would give anything to ride in one of those machines," I told my dad. In fact, I pleaded for months with my folks to take me to Manistee on the Fourth of July, 1932 and let me spend the two weeks' wages I'd earned working in the drug store to ride in a Ford tri-motored airship. It had a corrugated metal skin with wicker seats. I'm sure my Dad thought that I had lost all good reasoning for wanting to leave the ground in a machine such as that. I held my breath for most of the twenty-minute trip into the skies above Manistee Lake.

Meanwhile, the last three months wasn't what I had in mind, to fly weather recon, then two aborted and eight completed missions in seventy-two days, then being shot down and captured. This trip to a stalag was never in the plans. As the train rumbled on toward Linz the engineer seemed to take great pleasure in switching rails. He continued to bump and jar us out of our spots on the floor, or on the bench, throughout the journey. I jerked back and forth at the waist with each jar of the train.

At first the thought of leaving Dulag Luft was a dream come true: no more incarceration in Federal Prison or at the interrogation center. Rolfing and I hadn't seen eye to eye and it wasn't good to crawl too far under the skin of someone in his position. But every click of the rails took the train away from England and farther away from home. The American flyers onboard had been given a one-way ticket. They could only guess how long it would be before, or if, they would return. The three days it took to reach Krems were long ones, but the sixteen months that lay ahead were going to be a good deal longer. Our destination was Stalag 17B, the notorious German POW camp that earned the dubious reputation as the worst POW camp in the German system.

From all outward appearances the boxcar was similar to boxcars in the States, only two-thirds in length. The inside had the "luxury" of a bench all around the perimeter. The floor was lightly covered with straw. I had watched cattle being loaded onto a railroad car like this when I was a youngster. At the marshalling yard in Frankfurt the American POWs looked just like those cattle. Within an hour from the time we boarded, the locomotive with its other boxcars backed into ours with a strong jolt. Before leaving the marshalling yard ours, in turn, backed into more railroad cars. Once assembled the train rolled out of Frankfurt.

Each POW immediately staked out a spot on the bench or floor. Charlie, Steiler, Comer, Wingate and McDowell had all been ushered in ahead of me. By the time I got on the only spot left was on the thinly straw-lined floor along with half the other men. I sat down near Charlie and McDowell.

I was telling them about my visits to Rolfing's office. McDowell looked at me in disbelief and said, "You got to be kidding. Rolfing interrogated me too. When I was in his office he showed me a book entitled, *The 91st Bomb Group*. Rolfing knew the answers to every one of the questions he was asking you, Ras. He knew the name of our induction center, every airbase we'd gone, including Cal Flyers and specialty tech school at Douglas Aircraft Plant. He knew about Laredo Gunnery School and flying school at Moses Lake. Rolfing knew the exact order of every stop in our training."

I was dumbfounded.

"Rolfing even showed me a picture of our headquarters in Bassingbourn."

It was hard to believe what McDowell was saying. "That means I hadn't withheld anything from Rolfing that he didn't already know," I finally said. "Then the only thing he was asking about, and didn't get an answer to, was where the B-17s were coming from." I sat there for a moment and thought about how Rolfing had fooled me. "Oh well, he still seemed pretty pissed off that I didn't answer his questions."

"Paige Gillerman," a hand stuck out in my direction. Paige was sitting on the floor next to me. He was a slightly built guy of five feet four inches. With his red hair and freckles, he looked all of fifteen. I wonder if he had lied about his age when he enlisted. Paige too, had been a gunner on a B-17. Everyone in Stalag 17B, who got to know Paige, liked him. He shined up to the other soldiers, like a little brother. He was an agreeable fellow. Whenever we asked if he wanted to do something, his stock answer was, "I don't care."

"Bill Rasmussen. It doesn't look like we're going first cabin on this ride," I responded, shaking his hand. "Where're you from?"

Whenever Paige spoke his words came out fast. "Chicago, but I didn't grow up in a real home. I lived in an orphanage with a lot of other kids. I was glad to enlist but I never thought about going to prison." Paige's first statement told me how important home was to him. He was more insecure than the other flyers who had been captured, because he hadn't developed the inner strength one gets growing up in a family.

"You gotta dog?" Paige had lots of questions for me. I must have told him my whole life's story during that first night.

"Yeah." I answered. "His name is Jarvis. He always runs away."

A few moments later he asked, "Ever go on a real trip with your family?"

"Went to the circus. It stopped in Manistee, not Fountain where I grew up. I remember Oley Hansen, one of my brother's friends, saying that we weren't ever gettin' to see the circus because it didn't stop in our hometown. Our folks had refused to make the thirty or so mile journey to Manistee. Oley and my brother and I were chewing on long straw stems from dried grass and could not imagine what could be a more important thing for our parents to do than to take us to see the circus acts. Then, when I was eleven, Oley's folks piled us all into the back of their pickup and drove to Manistee to see the elephants and bears and the trapeze artists. You'd thought we'd died and gone to heaven."

There was no food to eat on the transport train. That guard in Federal prison proved himself right again. What I would have done to have that bowl of potato soup right then. There was no water either. Survival lesson 101 at Moses Lake had been a lecture on the importance of keeping hydrated. "If you are shot down behind enemy lines," the instructor said, "your first priority is to evade capture, your second is to obtain water. Under no circumstances are you to become dehydrated." The flyers who had contracted dysentery were losing a lot of fluid and didn't have access to water.

The Germans did provide one convenience: a six-gallon pail that served as porta-john. Many of the POWs had contracted dysentery and were already losing strength due to dehydration. Over the next thirty-six hours, the porta-john filled until it was of no value. The prison train advanced slowly, sidetracking often to let the scheduled German troop trains pass. It bumped down the track, and as it did, the contents of the pail splashed out. The boxcar soon smelled like a latrine and became filthy. Those who sat on the floor or tried to sleep could only hope that the waste they had to cope with was their own. The unsanitary conditions were yet another way for the Germans to try to break down morale. If we had no spirit left, then our will to fight back would certainly vanish.

Warren Graham was another ex-flyer I met on the way. He squatted on the floor a few feet away. Warren had been a tail-gunner on a B-24 that had been shot down near Berlin. He had grown up on a farm in Idaho and had built a lot of muscle as a result of the hard farm work. His neck must have been a size eighteen. Besides being the strongest man I had ever met, he had a good sense of humor. On the train ride he was totally unflappable. "This is worse than the barnyard back home," he said. "We're the ones penned up, just like we did to our pigs. Huh, huh, huh, huh." Graham spoke in the deepest voice I ever heard. He often finished what he was saying by laughing to himself with that "Huh, huh, huh, huh." I looked at him and wondered if it wasn't a family trait, perhaps something that his father had done and Graham picked it up. Whatever the reason, he was a charming man and not one to make fun of. The cold did not seem to bother Graham as much as it did the other soldiers. I guessed that his upbringing put him outside on many a winter's day, so he had gotten used to being cold. I could picture him outside their family's barn back in Idaho at five o'clock on a cold winter's morning. I could see his mom yelling at him to bundle up when he went out to milk the cows before breakfast.

"Put on your coat and hat," she would fuss at him. Graham was the kind of boy who would enjoy teasing his Mom. He'd just smile and keep on walking.

Late into our second day, the train came to a halt. We had arrived at Linz, Austria, sixty miles and still a day's travel west of Krems. After an hour, German voices came closer to our boxcar until finally the lock released and the door slid back. "Clean out this mess and you will be provided with food, water and clean straw," one of the German soldiers barked in English.

Those of us who were able helped with the cleaning program, but several soldiers were too ill. They needed to be carried out of the boxcar and laid on the ground. As this was being done, I glanced up and down the train. It consisted of some twenty boxcars, but it was impossible to determine if there were other POWs in any of them. All their doors remained closed. Someone was inside of them but it was only a guess as to whom. They were very quiet and must have been told to remain silent. After all the ex-flyers were out of the boxcar and the old straw had been replaced with new, the Germans gave us black bread, barley soup, and as much water as we could drink.

The guards then turned their attention elsewhere. After watching for several minutes I decided it was the right time for a boy like me to start for home. In retrospect, I'm not sure what was going through my head at the time. Falleck and I hadn't made it very far three weeks earlier and that was at a time when we had all our strength, as well as provisions and currency for more provisions. What chance was there starting from a marshalling yard in Austria? We didn't even have military issue boots, only the wooden clogs that were impossible to run in.

"Let's go," I said to two of the other soldiers who had helped carry one of our weak comrades off the train. The three of us took off across the thirty pairs of railroad tracks. Our freedom was probably the shortest on record because the guards began to fire at us before we got halfway across the yard. When you're the intended target, rapid bursts of machine gun fire are a quick jerk back to reality. The three of us fell prone on the ground next to a railroad track and tried to make ourselves the smallest target possible. Believe me, trying to hide behind a railroad track is not easy. One of the guards fired a few more rounds over our heads. Why the Germans did not kill us, I am still uncertain. Perhaps they were under orders to get all of the flyers to Stalag 17B.

"Take them to the end of the marshalling yard," a Gestapo agent who headed our captors ordered in English. "They will be charged with sabotage."

"Not smart," I whispered to myself. There was no point in being angry now. I had already learned the value of conserving strength and this was one of those times. The three of us were shackled together and marched a mile down a road to just outside Linz. The guards shoved us inside a vacant concrete building with very little light. We remained there for four hours, not sure of our fate. Then the guards came back.

"March," an English speaking guard commanded. Back down the road we marched, chained together. Once we were at the marshalling yard, the chains were unshackled.

"Up the plank!" the guard shouted. The wooden plank led to the same boxcar where we had been before our big break. We found an open place on the floor and sat down.

"Not smart, Ras," Charlie said.

"Yeah, I thought that was it for you guys," Graham bellowed out. "Huh, huh, huh, huh."

"So did I," one of the POWs who I had been shackled with responded.

Once the doors were closed, we told the rest of the former flyers about our escape attempt. Now that it was obvious how silly the escape attempt had been, everyone got a good laugh out of it, especially Graham. After two more hours of sitting, the train started moving.

Three days outside of Frankfurt, and one day east of Linz, the train screeched to a halt. We had reached Krems in northeast Austria, two hundred eighty-one miles from the German border. We still had a mile and a half march to Stalag 17B and sixteen months of living in hell.

11

Stalag 17B

IT WAS CHRISTMAS AFTERNOON 1943 AND WE WERE ON A sidetrack of the marshalling yard in Krems, Austria.

"Here they come," Paige said. Voices outside and the unlocking of the boxcar held us in suspense. "I need to do is get out of mess and get some fresh air." Several days had passed without the benefit of a bath, shave or change of clothes.

Even Charlie and Steiler were hard to recognize. "You two ain't going to a box social looking like that," I said while we waited to get off the train. Besides being filthy, Charlie's hair was greased down and whiskers darkened his face. Steiler's facial skin, broken from frostbite, hadn't healed. As the door slid open, the Germans greeted us with the same demands that had greeted us at Linz.

"Get out," a guard yelled. A squad of thirty German soldiers greeted the sixty-seven ex-flyers as we disembarked the train.

Using rifle butts, the guards shoved us out of the boxcar. The day was bright and sunny and our eyes squinted until they adjusted to the winter day. The marshalling yard in Krems was smaller than the one in Linz. Krems was a much smaller Austrian town, with a population of around 15,000. There was very little going on. No other trains rolled through the station.

"Look around, this place hasn't been hit yet," Charlie said. Surprisingly, most of the single story buildings around the yard had been spared the ravages of bombing. But it would only be a matter of time before this marshalling yard made the target list.

After all the POWs were out of the boxcar, including those who were unable to walk without help, the guards herded us across the tracks to a snow-covered street and what turned out to be a one and a half mile hike.

"Nothing around here looks like it's a holiday season," Steiler said. No decorations hung in the town. No one was on their way to visit their family for Christmas dinner. The single car we saw had only a driver.

Waiting at the end of our trek was a recently vacated concentration camp, newly named Stalag 17B, one of seventy-eight German POW camps and one of the most infamous. The buildings had been built to house political internees. We didn't know what had happened to them. The compound was divided into sections and surrounded by a barbed wire fence, and six feet inside the fence by a "warning wire."

"You are not allowed to cross or touch the warning wire," the guard announced on our arrival. "You will be shot without warning if you do." Fencing also separated prisoners of different nationalities. The American section consisted of sixteen barracks at the east end designated as areas four, five, eight and nine. Guard towers were located around the entire perimeter. Outside the perimeter, on the east end of the prison, surrounded by trees, was the burial ground for soldiers who died while in Stalag 17B. When we arrived we became kriegsgefangenens, or prisoners of war, kriegies for short. Jerry handed each of us a new dog tag with a German serial number. Mine was 100483.

"You will never forget your number," the guard warned. "Now get in line for processing." Our mug shots were taken, front and side view.

In all there were over 30,000 prisoners in Stalag 17B. Four thousand two hundred were American Air Force sergeants, the flyers who had played such a crucial role in destroying the Nazis' plans for world domination. One thousand three hundred American flyers had been relocated to Stalag 17B from Stalag 7A in Moosburg, Germany three months before my arrival. There were Russians, who the Germans hated, and Italians, who the Germans despised after they signed the armistice with the Allies two months before our arrival. There were Serbs, Slovaks, French, Poles, and a few British as well.

The Commandant was Oberst Kuhn. Kuhn was Wehrmacht and hated the American flyers even more than the other prisoners at Stalag. He was a hard-line German officer who succeeded in making our lives as miserable as possible. Many cases were recorded of the kriegies being struck by pistols and rifle butts, even bayonets. Because the Germans thought the American flyers knew the pipeline of the B-17s and B-24s, some of them were selected for "interrogation" and never returned. Minor infractions of the rules got a soldier shot in 1943 and 1944. They became tolerated only toward the end of the war when the Germans realized the inevitable outcome and what our value was when they bargained with the Allies. They also realized late in the war that the American Army would hold them responsible for their atrocities.

"I'll bet there's not a German officer alive who doesn't see our tanks in his nightmares," I told Charlie when we entered the gate at Stalag 17B. "I know that one day they'll come for us."

"You are to shower and be deloused," the guard ordered after we entered the camp. Getting a shower was music to our ears. Maybe it had been all right to dream of sitting in a warm tub with soap bubbles and a sponge to scrub down with. It sounded like the next best thing to a homemade meal. The guard barked out his next command, "You will remove all your clothing and stand in line for a haircut before the shower." The Germans intended on gassing our clothes in order to kill any mites.

Our barber turned out to be a civilian prisoner who shaved our heads. "This is something I haven't done before," I said to Charlie who was standing behind me. "It's the first time anyone has cut my hair when I haven't been wearing anything!"

"Yeah," Charlie said. "And the first time we get our hair cut while we freeze our sorry asses."

We were on to the next line. "Dam," Charlie yelled after our pubic hair had been shaved. "This stuff burns like hell." Our scrotums were being painted with a thin black liquid to kill lice. It was some sort of petroleum product that burned for the next two days. Next, we were ushered to a building twenty by thirty feet with showerheads around the perimeter. It had two temperature settings—cold and colder. To tolerate the icy water, all the boys danced and yelled during the two-minute icy shower.

Then it was on to an adjoining building to pick up our uniforms. "Open the doors and claim your uniforms," the guard ordered once we were inside. When the chamber doors opened, those poor souls near them passed out from the fumes.

"Pull them outside," one of our soldiers yelled. Quickly, the unconscious kriegies were pulled away from the deadly fumes. The guards got a big laugh as sixty-seven bareheaded and bare-butt GIs thrashed around trying to find their clothes when the temperature was a chilly eighteen degrees. It had been anything but a refreshing shower and change of clothes.

"Can you believe this?" Graham said. "Our clothes are still filthy." Graham had a big smile on his face. He was standing on the edge of the circle of men with his clothes already on. He turned to a guard and kept saying "thank you" in a mocking style. The guard nodded his head and actually smiled back.

After this we were marched off across the compound to our prison. I never knew anyone who had been in jail in America. Stalag was nothing like what I imagined our jails to be like. Prisoners in American jails and prisoners of war in American prison camps received shelter, heat, adequate food, sanitary conditions and medical attention when needed. The Germans argued that the standards at Stalag 17B met those established by the Geneva Convention and that Stalag 17B was similar to American POW camps. American soldiers at Stalag 17B received none of those basic human necessities. Unless you got a package from home, even daily toilet items that were taken for granted, toothpaste, toothbrush, shaving cream, razors, toilet paper and soap were non-existent.

We were fortunate that four French doctors and one dentist had been captured and sent to Stalag 17B. Under the circumstances, they did an outstanding job caring for the sick and injured Americans. They pulled teeth, set bones, and even took out an appendix. Captain Stephen Kane, a priest, was our only chaplain. He served all denominations and all the American soldiers had a good rapport with him, no matter what their faith. The ex-flyers prayed with Father Kane frequently. On Sundays, Father Kane held services for all denominations. The Germans watched him very closely, but in my entire time in Stalag the Germans never bothered Father Kane. At times I thought they were afraid of him.

My assigned quarters at Stalag 17B was barracks 18A.

"Will you look at these digs?" Charlie said when we got to the barracks. We were located in the "new air force camp" at the east end of the Stalag that had been opened in November 1943. Each of the barracks was built in two sections with a washroom in between.

The washroom was for washing and nothing else, no shaving, no toilet, just washing. Even though it was "verboten," we sometimes hung our wash on the warning wire. The washroom was divided into two rooms, one with a concrete tank to store water, the other with a metal trough and an overhead pipe with holes drilled for a water outlet. The guards turned the water on between seven and eight in the morning, between noon and one in the afternoon and in the evening starting at five o'clock. They left it on for most of the evening until the lights went out. The guards used water as another means to hold something over us: if they chose not to, they wouldn't turn it on at all. My guess was that fresh water, like everything else, was a declining resource for the Nazis. They simply could not afford to waste it on kriegies and certainly could not afford to heat it.

In the front and rear sections of the barracks were fourteen bunks. Each bunk had three shelves, sheets of wood that held four men. There were twelve men to a bunk and fourteen bunks to a section. Each barracks averaged two hundred forty POWs.

"Charlie," I said after our barrack's only light bulb was out the first night.

"Yea, Ras?"

"It's going to take me a long time to own up to the fact that I'm sleeping in the same bed with three other men."

Each barracks had a central heating system, a small open stove. The problem was that it didn't come with any fuel. The Germans provided the facade of heating the barracks for the singular purpose of passing inspections. In the sixteen months I was at Stalag, our barracks was issued a small supply of coal only twice. With no fuel and missing windowpanes, it was desirable to be one of the inside partners in your bunk. Heat from your sack mate helped you stay warm during the cold winter nights.

The Germans found other ways besides the filth, the cold, hunger, and their rules to make our lives miserable. Unsanitary conditions that were present throughout internment resulted in the POWs being covered with mites and lice. Everyone was covered with everything that crawled. You could see the small white lice on another GI's head. All the POWs got them. It didn't do any good to fret about them, or think about getting rid of them. POWs in Stalag were stuck with them.

In Stalag 17B, each kriegie got a blanket and a straw-filled burlap sack that served as a mattress. It was also filled with fleas. The fleas came from rats that woke you up at night when they gnawed at the foundation underneath the barracks, or worse yet, when they squealed once they got inside the barracks to look for food. The fleas jumped from the rats and got into the burlap sack and in our clothes. It didn't take much to figure out that the sacks were put to better use keeping us warm, even for a brief time, by burning them in the open stove. Once the fleas got on you, scores of them moved in formation, taking a bite every inch in their travels. To combat this, the kriegies learned to remove nothing upon retiring but their shoes. Those that had laces used them to tie their pant legs tight. Shirtsleeves were worn buttoned down tight and collars were buttoned as well. This didn't win the battle, but it was possible to slow the invasion down to a crawl. Fleabites led the long list of miseries of daily existence at Stalag 17B. Vitamin deficiency compounded the problem by keeping sores open for weeks on end. It was a must not to break the skin when you scratched a bite.

It was obvious that the Germans had no real plans to handle the waste management of 30,000 POWs. Health problems compounded the waste problems and the waste problems made for more unsanitary conditions. Dysentery resulted from the terrible sanitation conditions. At the end of the barracks was a night crapper, a hole in the ground. Between taps (when you retire) and reveille (when you rise), usually around nine at night and five-thirty in the morning, prisoners had to use the barrack's latrine.

"And I thought the crapper in our barracks was bad," Charlie lamented the first day we were in Stalag. "You ought to see the main latrine." In the middle of the American section was a "twenty-four holer."

"You need to step up close to pee," one of the kriegies told me on my first visit. "The next man may be barefoot."

Kriegies got used to sitting on the crapper because of frequent attacks of dysentery. Keeping clean in Stalag 17B, when you had diarrhea, was always a problem. Graham had the solution. "Just wipe with your left hand, and eat with your right. Huh, huh, huh, huh!"

"There needs to be some way to get the shit away from our barracks," Steiler said soon after we had arrived. The barrack's latrine had overflowed.

"We'll dig a ditch to the perimeter and let it flow away from the barracks," Graham said without any hesitation. It was a popular idea and everyone helped, digging it with empty tin cans. It helped carry the waste away toward the open field behind our barracks. We occasionally got use of a "honey wagon," a large barrel mounted on a wagon, pulled by a horse. A pump was attached to the back end of the barrel. The guards sometimes allowed the POWs to pump out overflowing latrines and haul the sewage out to a local potato patch to be scattered. But the latrines often overflowed, and the smell was terrible, especially in the warm summer months when the smell permeated the air.

What got my attention right away was the warning sign posted around the camp. If anything good could be said about Stalag, it was the good understanding of the rules that the Lageroffizier posted. The time limit when the GIs were allowed outside of their barracks was posted on the warning notice. No one was allowed out of their barracks between taps and reveille. The POWs had ample time to get inside their barracks after taps sounded, but not too much time. Generally, within fifteen minutes, all the kriegies were expected to be inside. The one exception to this rule was during air raids. Day or night, when the alarm sounded, the POWs had permission to run from the barracks and hide in trenches.

Roll call our first full day in Stalag came at six in the morning and lasted for several hours. It wasn't unusual to have roll call two or three times a day, keeping the POWs out in the cold or in the rain. Jerry called the POWs from two of the barracks, then two more, and so on. I saw how the kriegies fooled the guards on the first day when one of the smaller GIs stood on the feet of a taller soldier inside his overcoat. They never did catch on to this routine, but got really mad every time the number of POWs kept changing whenever the count was made. You laughed inside but didn't let any of the guards see you laughing at them.

On October 1, 1943, a B-24 Liberator was shot down on a raid over Vienna, Austria. Antiaircraft shells shattered the four-engine bomber and six of the ten men were killed when the ship crash-landed. Harold Shealian was a 24-year-old flyer from Chicago. He was the radio operator and a gunner. Hal was severely wounded in the explosion and had parachuted out. Both of his legs were badly wounded, one shattered. He was found by three Germans who wrapped him in his parachute in an attempt to stop the bleeding, then took him to a nearby hospital. Doctors pulled one hundred seven pieces of shrapnel from his body and plugged a large hole in the back of one of his legs. Still recovering from surgery, Shealian was transferred to Stalag 17B. I met him at that first roll call and we became good friends.

Hal was right behind me one day in line as we queued up to have the Germans check the serial numbers on our German dog tags.

"That soldier should not have to stand out here while you check his dog tag," I told the guard at the table. "He hasn't healed from his wounds and isn't going anywhere."

"Leave the area," the German guard ordered. When we were back in the barracks, talk was about our first impressions of Stalag. The conversation got around to Hal.

"Thanks for trying to let me sleep in but I'm getting stronger every day. I don't want to give them the satisfaction that they've stopped me from walking," he said.

Night came to Stalag with a life of its own. Each barracks had a single light bulb. When the light bulb was turned out, the camp took on a different face. Sleep came mostly from exhaustion and for short periods, especially during the first few months after we arrived. The ex-flyers didn't talk much at night; there wasn't anything left to talk about. It was far from quiet though. The guards enjoyed making noise. Heavy trucks came and went. The best noise came with the RAF bombers. The worse sound came from the rats.

On our first day in Stalag and the boys wanted to play a game of poker. "Let's ask the guards for a deck of cards," Charlie suggested. That wasn't going to happen.

Comer asked, "Can anyone draw a deck?"

McDowell announced to everyone that I liked to gamble. "Ras can make the deck the way it's supposed to look," he said. "He took our money playing poker back at Bassingbourn so he must know what the face cards look like."

"That so?" Graham asked. "Do you remember enough about the deck to make us one?"

"Poker?" I replied. "Is that where two's good and three's better? Well, I've played a hand or two. Mac's right, I did win a few hands.

What he forgot to say is that I'm the one who bought the beer after the game."

"Let's see, the Jack of Spades and Jack of Hearts each have one eye. The Jack of Hearts is the boy with the ax and is the only boy that gets to play with a weapon. Seems he grew up early. The only queen that looks to her left is the Queen of Spades; she's known to cheat by looking into the next guy's hand. In fact the whole spade family as well as the Jack of Clubs are trying to look into the hand of the guy on the left of you. The lady who loves you is the Queen of Hearts. She holds her flower straight up to give them to you, thinking that you might reward her with a big bet. Trust me, whenever you hold her, squeeze her tight and bet big. The King of Hearts committed suicide by sticking his sword right into his noggin. Seems he didn't like his lady picking flowers for you. The man with the ax is the King of Diamonds. Never trust the man with the ax. He tries to distract you by waving his little pinkies at you while he lowers his ax. He's the only guy that shows you his hands. If someone else is holding the man with the ax, it's time to fold 'em. Both the black kings are swordsmen and hold their sword pointing due north. Yep, I've played enough to remember what they look like. I even got a game to teach you. It's called Ol' Ras wins."

"Well then, you get the job of making the deck of cards for the camp. Huh, huh, huh, huh," Graham laughed. You'd have thought that Graham had settled every problem in Stalag. I made the cards from paper that was ripped from the Red Cross parcels. As it turned out, the cards were copied many times over and used all over the camp. Hal and I later used them to play bridge and pinochle. I managed to pick up some chocolate bars and cigarettes in a few poker games and used them as trading items. The Red Cross provided regular playing cards in July 1944. But even then, there weren't enough to go around.

Another one of my friends was Ben Phelper. Ben had been an artist for Disney Studios before the war. During that first week in Stalag Ben had got a hold of quite a prize. "Look what I've got," he announced to me. Ben had managed to trade cigarettes for a very small camera that used film about a half an inch wide and a couple of inches long.

Italian prisoners were allowed to take a few personal items with them to Stalag 17B; the camera and two rolls of film were among them.

"It looks like something you better be awfully careful with, Ben," I told him. "The Germans will accuse you of being a spy if they catch you with it."

I'm taking as many pictures as I can," he said. "If we ever get out of this place we'll have something to show everyone." Ben managed to take a number of pictures in Stalag and kept his camera secret the whole time we were there.

We were a strange looking group of American flyers after our first week in Stalag 17B, wearing hand-me-down uniforms. As time went on, we looked worse. Our beards grew longer by the day. We got a shower about every six weeks. The guards allowed us three visits to the local delousing area during the next sixteen months. Each time we got our scrotums painted black and they burned for days just like they had the first time.

Our main mission in Stalag 17B was survival. Except for injuries and dysentery, all the ex-flyers started internment in the same excellent health as they were when accepted as members of an aircrew. But as the fortunes of war turned against the Nazis, the German's feelings of disdain toward the captured flyers turned to hatred. The bombings of Fortress Europe during the previous year and a half had been devastating to the German war effort and the civilian population. The German citizens viewed the bombing campaign as raids of terror against their homeland and the families of the German soldiers.

I remembered reading a book by Kenneth Roberts entitled *Oliver Wiswell*, a story of our own Revolutionary War. One chapter related the experiences of prisoners of war. After becoming a POW, I was sure the author was writing about Stalag 17B. The captured soldiers of 1776 had most of the same hardships as the WWII POWs. I also recalled reading in college about the Union troops at Andersonville who tried to survive notorious conditions. Now, eighty years later in Stalag, it was the American flyers who were in desperate conditions.

The human body can stand untold hardships, but your emotions can be the hardest thing to deal with. Fights often broke out over petty things. Such behavior was subdued in short order and in most all cases the parties involved ended up as friends. Some of our soldiers weren't so lucky. Some became consumed with hate and expended too much negative energy. I found out that there wasn't enough emotional energy to hate Stalag and the Germans at the same time. Hate has a brother: depression. Once a POW was spent emotionally and became depressed, then he withdrew into himself. His health suffered because the fight was out of him.

I didn't know Johnny Parks. Johnny was a tail gunner from New Mexico who tested the rules shortly after I arrived. Johnny had been shot down the past summer and, like his other crewmen, transferred from Stalag 7A to Stalag 17B in October 1943. After a few months, he just couldn't take being in prison any more. One night he ran from his barracks toward the guard tower. "Shoot me. Shoot me," he shouted at the guards. They did, and left his body, riddled with machine gun bullets, lying on the ground all night. Johnny was buried in the camp's cemetery the next morning. That convinced me very early in my stay in Stalag that the Germans meant what they said.

The German's goal for the captured American flyers was to demoralize them and force them into submission. It was their hope that by separating the enlisted flyers from the officers chaos would be the order of the day. It didn't happen. In Stalag 17B, the German guards were staring into the faces of 4,200 defiant American flyers who were anything but demoralized and who refused to give up hope of escaping and flying again. The captured flyers still had the discipline of good American soldiers and still held their heads high. The American flyers were too proud and too defiant to let the Germans feel they had broken them by putting them in prison.

Shortly after we arrived Father Kane told us that we were "4,000 men with broken wings."

"Father Kane's right, Charlie," I said that night. "It's true that the Nazis broke our wings but it is going be a long time before they break our collective spirit. It's going to be a long, long time before they break mine."

12

A Notice Home

ON DECEMBER 29, 1943, AT SIX IN THE MORNING BARRACKS 18 was notified of roll call. It was thirty degrees outside and still pitch black. We sauntered out of the barracks and queued up as our names were called off, sounding out our German serial number in turn. Morning meal was served at eight o'clock, a cup of warm water that was used to make coffee or tea.

Back in the barracks one of the POWs announced, "I'm writing down the words to some Christmas songs so we can all sing them later. Anyone know the words to *"O' Come All Ye Faithful?"* He had been at Stalag for a while and was trying to put a good face on it. The only answer came in the form of a lot of blank stares. For the ex-flyers in barracks 18 who had just arrived, singing Christmas songs was not what they had in mind. Everyone was much more intent on their own private thoughts of home and about loved ones.

I laid down in my sack and thought, by trying to sing Christmas carols, that GI was breaking up the boredom and keeping his spirits up. It was an idea that should not go to waste.

Being away from home at Christmas was bad enough; being in Stalag at Christmas was real tough, especially when everyone was just moping around. Not wanting to sing a Christmas carol to lighten up the day was not a good idea. Neither was it a good idea to stay in your sack talking to yourself when you're away from home at Christmas. I made a vow never to let the place get me down. Dealing with the Germans was one thing, fighting boredom was another, and it was something that could be dealt with. I had my family, my faith in God, and I knew in my heart that the Germans were not going to beat the Americans and the British. The destruction inflicted by the B-17s, B-24s and British bombers on the German ordnances was predicting the outcome of the war. It did not seem possible that the Germans could recover from the sustained bombing. After getting acclimated to this place, we would be more like the GI who wanted to sing those Christmas carols. Besides, singing songs and lightening up the day might crawl under the collective Germans' skin.

December 1, 1943 was the date the *Hell's Belle* was shot down. Ten days later the Secretary of War notified my parents, who were living in Cedar, Michigan, "with deep regret," that I was missing in action over Nazi Germany. On January 6, 1944, twenty-six days after that first notice arrived home, Dad was notified that my name had been mentioned in a German broadcast. The Federal Broadcast Intelligence Service of the Federal Communication Commission had obtained an unconfirmed report that "the name of Sgt William Edward Rasmussen has been mentioned in an enemy broadcast as a prisoner of war . . ." The Germans announced whom they had captured for propaganda purposes. All of this was, of course, unknown to me. I worried about what my parents were thinking, and hoped the letter I wrote them when I was in Dulag Luft had made it home.

On January 11, 1944, the Red Cross was able to confirm that I was indeed a prisoner. Another Western Union Telegram was sent to my dad from the Provost Marshall General's office. ("Those were long days, waiting for a notice. Each day was longer than the one before," Dad told me after I arrived home in July 1945. "Your Mom was convinced that you had been killed.")

The B-17F Flying Fortress had a length of 74 feet 9 inches, a wingspan of 103 feet 9 inches, and a height of 19 feet 1 inch. Four 1,200-horsepower Wright R1820-97 engines powered the B-17. Its gross weight was 56,000 pounds. It carried 2,780 gallons of fuel and had a range of 2,800 miles. Maximum cruising speed was 302 MPH. The B-17 carried an 8,000-pound payload of bombs. One nineteen hundred electrical motors provided internal power. A crew of ten manned the B-17. Armament consisted of eleven, .50-caliber Browning machine guns. (USAF Museum photograph)

Wally Waitre, Dick Rowlson and Bill Rasmussen were classmates at Cal Flyers and at specialty school at the Douglas Aircraft Plant. The photograph was taken outside the Carlton Hotel in July 1942.

CLASS OF 'OCT-'42 CALIFORNIA FLYERS SCHOOL OF AERONAUTICS:
Back Row: Earle St. Pere, Chicago, Ill.; Dick Rowlson, Somerset Center, Mich.; Jerry Heagney, Chicago, Ill.; Nick Dzamon, Chicago, Ill.; John Gilland, Comstock Park, Mich.; Clem Morgan, Chicago, Ill.; Ray Vliek, Decatur, Mich.; John Nelson, Chicago, Ill.

3rd Row: John Meyer, Pontiac, Mich.; Walter Wiatre, Chicago, Ill.; James Cramer, Mapleton, Minn.; Jerry Dupen, Rothberry, Mich.; Bill Rasmussen, Cedar, Mich.; Fred Striet, Aurora, Ill.; Art Mitchell, Greenup, Ill.

2nd Row: Howard Flemming, Marine City, Mich.; Dick Underwood, Detroit, Mich.; Homer Iseman, Chicago, Ill.; James Gatlin, Blue Mountain, Ark.; Lou Prough, Santa Monica, CA.; Stan Slowik, Chicago, Ill.; Nathan Kalver, Chicago, Ill.

1st Row: Dan Turner, Chicago, Ill.; Lester Oswald, Santa Monica, CA.; Mike Cousineau, Muskegon, Mich.; Vincent Vallent, Ottawa, Ill.; John Sufalko, Cicero, Ill.; Virgil Shaw, Kankakee, Ill.; Walter Albert, Momence, Ill.

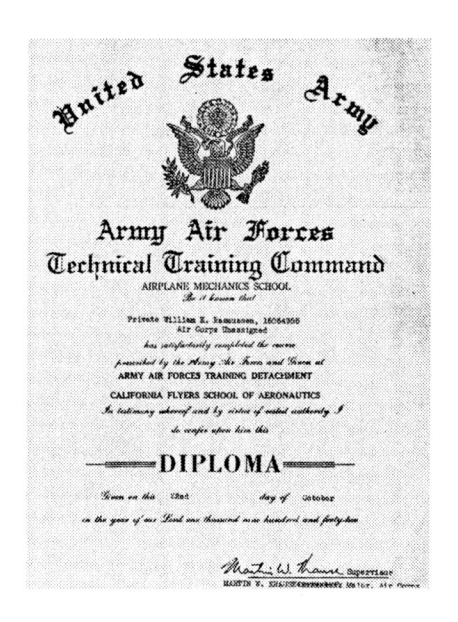

Flight crews had eighteen months of technical training before going overseas. At Cal Flyers crewmembers were taught airplane mechanics. Sgt. Rasmussen graduated from Cal Flyers in October 1942.

The crew of the B-17. *Top row*: Bert Steiler, top hatch gunner, radio operator; Harold Wingate, top turret gunner, flight engineer; Charles Quinn, pilot; John Hinda, right waist gunner, armament.
Center Row: Kenneth Falleck, co-pilot; Robert Hornbeck, navigator, nose gunner; Sidney Edelstein, bombardier, nose gunner; Charles Dyer, left waist gunner, engineer.
Front Row: Bill Rasmussen, ball turret gunner, engineer; Gerald McDowell, tail gunner, armament.
Not Pictured: Cecil Comer, right waist gunner. Cecil replaced John Hinda on December 1, 1943.

The Sperry Ball Turret is a globe of Plexiglas and metal four feet in diameter with twin .50-caliber machine guns. The ball turret hung from the belly of the B-17 by a mounting ring. During missions the ball turret gunner sat inside the rotating turret.

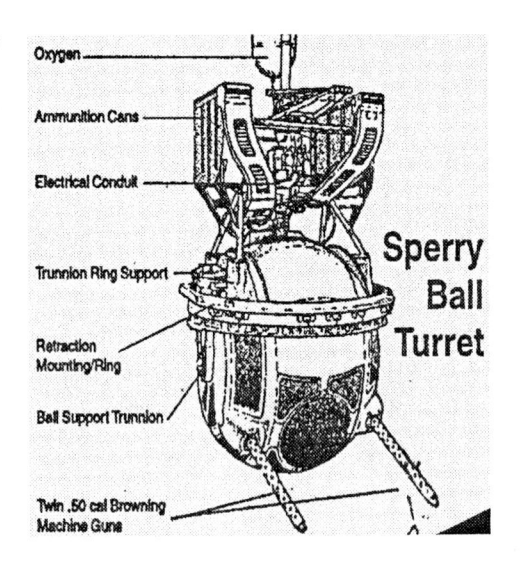

Sperry Ball Turret

- Oxygen
- Ammunition Cans
- Electrical Conduit
- Trunnion Ring Support
- Retraction Mounting/Ring
- Ball Support Trunnion
- Twin .50 cal Browning Machine Guns

Sgt. William E. Rasmussen. The photograph was taken on a visit home before going overseas in September 1943.

Our crew flew the *Anxious Angel* from Rochester, New York to Gander, Newfoundland, then on to Nuts Corner in Northern, Ireland. The "*Angel*" was a "G" series B-17 with the new chin turret.

After arriving in England we were assigned the *"079" Buccaneer* for our first bombing missions.

99

The damaged *"079" Buccaneer.* The photograph was taken after we returned from a mission to Bremen on November 26, 1943.

On the wing: 2nd Lt. Robert J. Hornbeck, navigator, Chicago, Ill; 2nd Lt. Charles Quinn, pilot, Phoenix, Arizona; 2nd Lt. Sidney Edelstein, bombardier, Brooklyn, N. Y.; and 2nd Lt. Kenneth W. Falleck, co-pilot, Greeley, Colorado.

The other members of the crew looking up at the wing from the ground: S/Sgt. Harold E. Wingate, engineer and top turret gunner, Baltimore, Md.; Sgt. Wm. E. Rasmussen, ball turret gunner and engineer, Cedar, Mich.; and S/Sgt. Bert A Stieler, radio operator and gunner, Albany, N.Y.

Members of the crew not shown are Sgt. Charles W. Dyer, engineer and left waist gunner, Spencer, Indiana; Sgt. John Hinda, right waist gunner and armorer, Pittsburgh, Pa.; and Sgt. Gerald E. McDowell, tail gunner and armorer, Merion, Pa.

The other five men who are not identified in the photograph were not part of the crew. (USAF Government photograph 27425C)

The *Hell's Belle* replaced the *'079' Buccaneer*. It was the last B-17 we flew in combat.

V. . . . MAIL sent just before our last mission on December 1, 1943 to my good friends the Scamehorns.

101

The *Hell's Belle* became a prize for the Germans. Four days after the ship crashed the German army dismantled the *Belle* and took her away for study. Curious civilians are pictured here examining the *Hell's Belle* in a field near Boich.

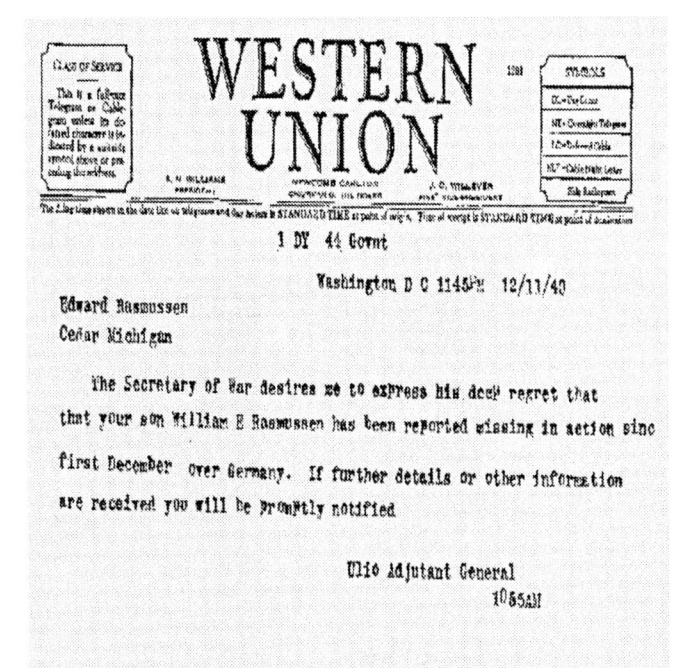

Rasmussen's parents received this telegram from the office of the Secretary of War ten days after the *Hell's Belle* was shot down.

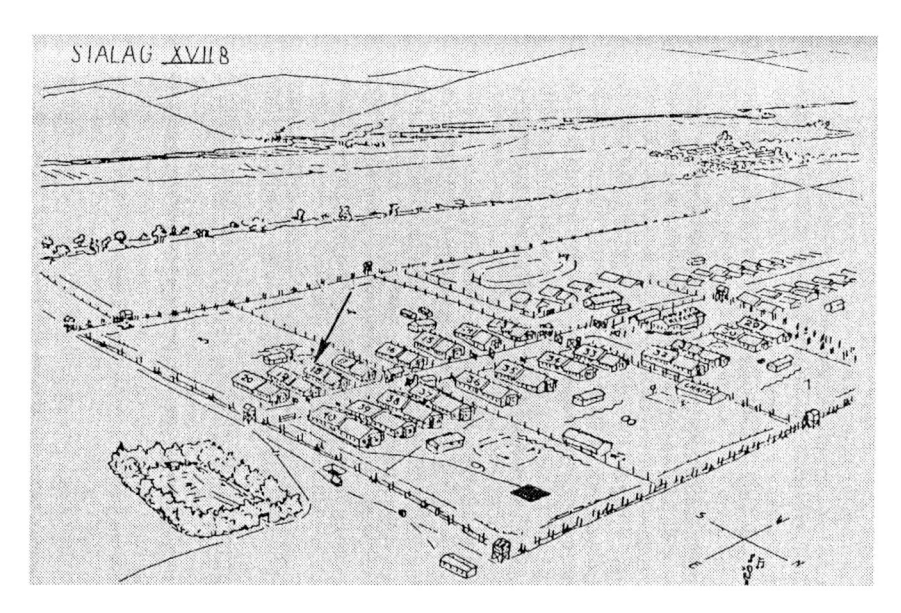

Four thousand two hundred captured American flyers were prisoners of war in Stalag 17B. (photograph by Ben H. Phelper)

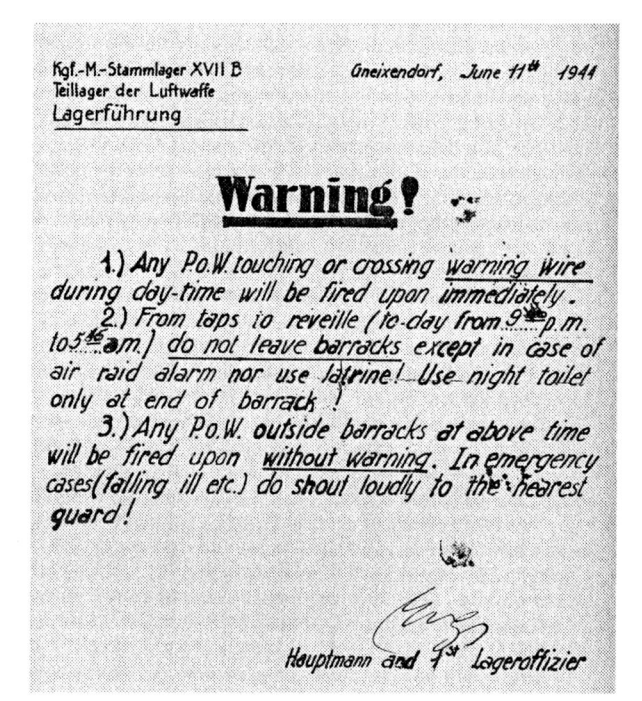

Kgf.-M.-Stammlager XVII B
Teillager der Luftwaffe
Lagerführung

Gneixendorf, June 11th 1944

Warning!

1.) Any P.o.W. touching or crossing warning wire during day-time will be fired upon immediately.

2.) From taps to reveille (to-day from 9 p.m. to 5 a.m.) do not leave barracks except in case of air raid alarm nor use latrine! Use night toilet only at end of barrack!

3.) Any P.o.W. outside barracks at above time will be fired upon without warning. In emergency cases (falling ill etc.) do shout loudly to the nearest guard!

Hauptmann and 1st Lageroffizier

One of the "welcoming signs" posted at Stalag 17B. The Germans made their points very clearly.

German guards patrolled between the rows of barracks in Stalag 17B.

The Germans piled mounds of tin cans next to the barbwire. If one of the POWs tried to escape, the racket coming from the cans alerted the guards.
(photograph by Ben H. Phelper)

Barracks 18A, section 5, Stalag 17B was Rasmussen's home for sixteen months. The front and rear sections of the barracks consisted of fourteen bunks, three shelves each, four men to a shelf. Each barracks averaged two hundred forty POWs. (photograph by Ben H. Phelper)

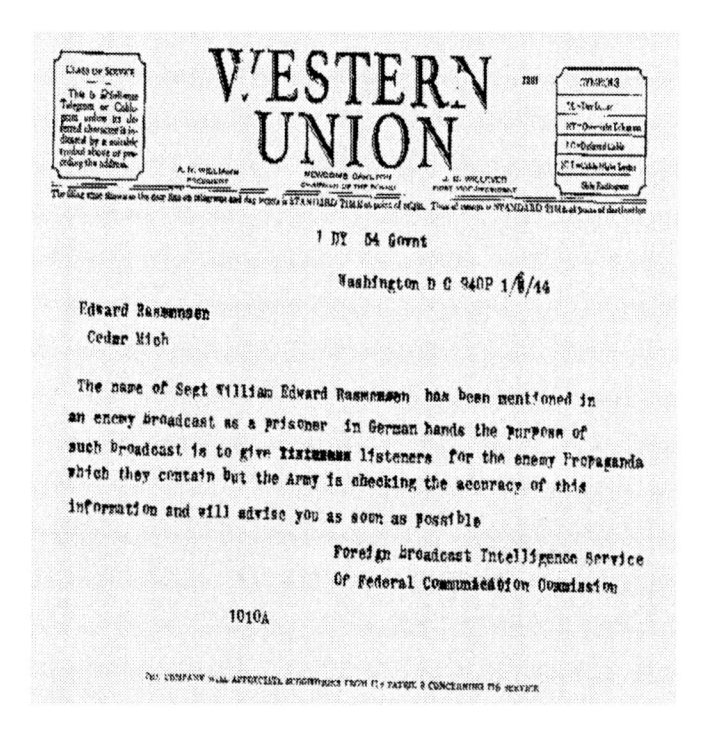

On January 6, 1944 Rasmussen's parents received a second telegram stating his name had been mentioned in a German radio broadcast. The notice came twenty-six days after they had been informed he was missing in action.

105

The main latrine in the camp was a "24-holer." (photograph by Ben H. Phelper)

When the latrine overflowed, the guards would sometimes send around a horse drawn "honey wagon" for the POWs to pump out the sewage. Once the "honey wagon" was full, it was pulled out outside the compound and the sewage dumped. (photograph by Ben H. Phelper)

POWs carried soup in the "chow tub" from the compound's kitchen to their barracks, one hundred thirty-six men to a tub, one dipper per man. (photograph by Ben H. Phelper)

The POWs shoveled garbage onto the horse-drawn trash wagon. One POW tried to escape by being buried under a pile of rubbish. (photograph by Ben H. Phelper)

Captain Father Kane was captured in North Africa and sent to Stalag 17B. The POWs constructed the chapel for him to minister. (photograph by Ben H. Phelper)

American POWs formed in military style and saluted whenever a coffin was carried away with one of their own. (photograph by Ben H. Phelper)

13

Some Grub to Eat

PRISON RATIONS LEFT A LOT TO BE DESIRED, BOTH IN QUANTITY and quality. In January 1944, just after my arrival in Stalag, the Germans cut our rations in half, claiming that the POWs had adequate food from the Red Cross parcels along with the food they provided.

A typical day's diet started with a cup of hot water in the morning. A lot of the men didn't bother to stand in line to get theirs. I always got mine and made coffee with it. Others used it for shaving. At noon and at night we got small portions of thin soup. Occasionally at night, we got something solid to eat. If the guards got a horse for their rations, then we got the head. If they got fish, usually salmon, we got the heads to make soup; the luckiest GI got the eyes. In fact, we called it "fish-eye soup." It was rare to get anything solid that was edible such as a piece of meat. It wasn't so rare to get something solid that wasn't edible, such as a tooth. Sometimes the Germans threw in two potatoes to boil with our main meal; broth that the spuds were boiled in made the soup. On Saturdays and Sundays our guards didn't issue the hot water and didn't bother providing us with an evening meal unless the Red Cross or the Swiss observers were in camp. They were there about every three months. Most of us never saw them.

Once a week we received two slices of black bread. The kriegies liked to joke a lot about the black bread. "Closest thing to wood of anything I've ever eaten," Charlie used to say. "It must have been baked before we ever got to this place and saved for us." Truth is, it wasn't that bad when you were hungry and softened it by soaking it in soup or tea.

Just about anything made soup including beets, rutabaga, potatoes and vegetables. In fact, there was a period when we had turnip soup every day for a whole month. Once in a while, vegetables that were beyond use to the Germans because of their spoilage were served to the POWs. The ingredients used for our meals soon convinced me that the best way to eat was to sit in a dark corner of our barracks and not think about what I was eating.

"I remember my favorite soup back home," I told Charlie the first time in Stalag when I heard what the boys were making. "Mom liked to make tomato soup. It was thick and made from milk the milkman delivered to our door twice each week. We skimmed the cream off the top and whatever Mom wasn't saving for her coffee was added to the soup. In the summer we took the reddest tomatoes, picked right off our own tomato plants, diced them, and added the pieces right into the mixture to make double tomato soup. Just add a little salt and pepper and have it with crackers and you had a meal." Soup in Stalag didn't make a meal. Sometimes it even made the kriegies sick.

The soup was made in the camp kitchen by some of our prisoners and then distributed to each barracks in a large chow tub. At the barracks it was divided among the POWs, one dipper per man. One tub served one hundred thirty-six men. Worms and bugs on the vegetables were included, free of charge. If anything in the soup made it objectionable for one of the kriegies to eat, then the next man got his share.

I didn't eat worms, but some of the other prisoners did. They didn't seem any the worse for it either. "Hey Charlie," I said as we ate our first rutabaga soup. "Look at those slimy little critters floating on top of your bowl. It looks like you got some real grub to eat." They were white cabbageworms floating on top the rutabaga soup. I got a good laugh out of it even if Charlie didn't.

One of the better meals the POWs prepared was barley soup, made by simmering the barley for a couple of hours. When the Germans gave our "chefs" salt to add to the soup, it became a real treat.

The best day of the week was when a Red Cross parcel came. Under the circumstances, the Red Cross was doing the best job they could. These parcels were taken to the camp kitchen before they were distributed to the men. The ex-flyers who were in Stalag 7A got parcels on any day the parcel arrived. No matter when the parcels were delivered to Stalag 17B, they were only distributed on Fridays. Those days were referred to as "pay day." A parcel itself provided better things to eat than anything else in camp but was meant to supplement other foods. One man could subside on the parcel for one week, at ten percent over starvation. Most of time the contents consisted of one can of powdered milk, one can of Spam or corned beef, one package of raisins or prunes, one can of oleo margarine, one can of concentrated orange pulp, one can of liver paste, one small box of crackers, two "D" bars (concentrated chocolate), seven ascorbic acid tablets (vitamin C used to prevent scurvy), one small box of sugar cubes, and one can of powdered coffee. When the raisins and prunes were stewed they tasted quite good. Five packs of cigarettes were also included and were very valuable as a tradable item.

The Germans kept a great number of the parcels that were destined for us, most often by not letting them be delivered to Stalag in the first place. Once, the German guards broke into the kitchen and stole three hundred Red Cross parcels and a few hundred packs of cigarettes. The Red Cross said that over 42,000 parcels were shipped to Stalag 17B in May 1944, enough for ten weeks, one per man per week. But in reality, because the guards took so many, one parcel had to be divided between two, three or four POWs each week.

The Germans punctured holes in all the canned goods with a bayonet before the food was issued to us. They confiscated and enjoyed any cans of food found unpunctured. "They're trying to prevent storage of any of the food," one of the kriegies who had been at Stalag 7B told me. "Stored food can be used during an escape. The only way to preserve the canned supplies is to plug the hole with margarine."

After opening one of the preserved cans we scraped off as little of the spoiled portion as possible and rationed the remainder. This would never have passed our food inspectors back home. Bacteria acted on putrefying foodstuffs and produced toxins. When the kriegies were hungry enough, they ate anything including spoiled foodstuffs and as a result, often got sick. Scores of the ex-flyers continually battled ptomaine poisoning after eating decaying food.

Everything had value in Stalag, even the empty cans. Empty cans had to be turned in. On "pay days," any POW who did not throw more than two or three cans into the bin had to go back and get more or the guards did not let him get into the parcel line. Other cans made the ceiling of our barracks look like a dump. They were hung below every spot that leaked rain. Some of the barracks had late model spigots in the washrooms; others were very old. Punching holes in the tin cans and hanging them from the faucets created a shower spigot. During the first few months at Stalag no one was issued any eating utensils. It was amazing to see how Yankee ingenuity transformed some of these cans into a variation of spoons and forks. It wasn't until April 1944 that the Germans issued a bowl and spoon to every third kriegie. By then most of us had made a bowl from the powdered milk can, a drinking mug from the margarine can and had already made a fork and spoon.

The German guards found a use for empty cans too. They piled them next to the fences. That way, if one of our soldiers was trying to cut his way through the barbwire, the guards could hear the cans tumbling about.

There was even a garbage hut at Stalag where refuse from the kitchen was thrown. "It's hard to believe what I just saw," Charlie told me our first full day in Stalag. "A few of our guys have been digging through the garbage to see if anything edible has been thrown out. One of the boys got "lucky" and found a rotten potato to dine on. He actually ate it."

"Rouse. You will take all the belongings that you desire to keep and assemble outside the compound." The command came from a German guard a week after I arrived.

"They must be transferring us to another camp," Graham said as we walked through the gate. Instead, when we were all outside the Germans ransacked our barracks, searching for anything of value. They repeated this again the following day. The third day when the Germans issued the same command most of us assembled outside the compound leaving our meager belongings behind. We didn't think they were after the food that had already been issued to us. That was what the Germans were waiting for. When they searched our barracks the third time, they took whatever they wanted, including the foodstuffs that were left behind. If we didn't carry it with us, they laid claim to it.

In Stalag, every day was a challenge.

14

The Cemetery

THE SKY STAYED GRAY ALL DAY ON THE 18TH OF FEBRUARY 1944, a very depressing gray. It was the contagious type of depression that spread to most of the men. An icy snow was falling. Two roll calls didn't help matters. As the ex-flyers stood in line for the second roll call, the cold wind that was racing between the barracks grabbed the icy snow and hurled it like darts at the POWs. Tempers ran thin and each man was better left alone rather than trying to engage him in conversation. On any other of winter's days those same snowflakes drifted endlessly, cautiously eyeing a spot to perch on the roofs of the wooden barracks. On this day the ground was covered with a layer of frozen, crusty snow, dirtied by the POW's endless trampling over it. It was the kind of frozen snow that made a loud sandpaper sound when we marched over it and was now covered with an icy skin. The wind was not about to let the new crystals carpet Stalag with a clean white blanket. Nothing in Stalag was clean, not even a blanket of freshly fallen snow. It was just the way things were in Stalag.

I got chilblains," Comer said as he came into the barracks from roll call. The winter in Stalag was similar to winter in northern Michigan. Fingers and toes sometimes swelled because they got too cold and broke open. If the chilblains were bad enough, infection sat in. "There's not much you can do other than keep your fingers as warm as possible and hope that they don't split open and get infected," Charlie told him.

Every day in Stalag, regardless of the weather, at least three of the Italian or Russian prisoners died. There weren't any body bags so the corpses were wrapped in heavy paper and carried on a stretcher by their weak comrades on their final journey. It was about half a mile from their section in Stalag to their section of the cemetery at the east end of the compound. As I mentioned, the Germans did not have much love for the Italians since they had surrendered to the West in September 1943. The Germans despised the Russians and weren't about to give them a soldier's burial, let alone have a funeral. There was no coffin for these dead soldiers, no honor guard and no fifteen-gun salute for a fallen comrade. The Nazis buried the dead Italians or Russians without any recognition that they had died as soldiers.

Also as I mentioned, the cemetery was located past the American section of Stalag. It was outside the fence and surrounded by a heavy belt of trees mixed in with tangled bushes. The Russians, Italians, French, Serb and Americans all had their own section in the graveyard. There were enough dead Russian and Italian POWs to densely populate their section of the cemetery. On every one of these winter mornings and later, as it turned out each morning of every season, a new procession marched by, the dead soldiers wrapped in paper, carried on the stretcher by his comrades and accompanied by German guards. Each morning we could watch them march by our barracks on the way to the end of the compound, out the gate to the waiting graveyard. The cemetery loomed forever outside the compound like a beckoning menace. It was one invitation I promised myself I would never accept.

No one in the procession said anything on February 18 as they marched by. After witnessing this daily event during my first few weeks in Stalag, it no longer grabbed my attention. I just happened to be outside our barracks' door mid-morning after the second roll call when a Russian contingent carrying three wrapped corpses marched by. I was surprised that on such a cold, miserable day those three graves had to be dug and their comrades laid to rest. Why couldn't they be wrapped in paper, left out in the cold and buried the next day? The German guards looked none too happy about the duty that they had drawn and were sure to take it out on the Russian soldiers who drew double duty as pallbearers and undertakers.

When an American soldier died of natural causes and was buried, the Germans gave a military gun salute to the fallen soldier. The British and the French also got funerals. The fallen American flyers were put in a coffin draped in the flag. The casket was made of heavy wood and was supported by a heavy four by four stand that took eight big soldiers to hoist it on their shoulders. The coffin was carried to the cemetery and the GI laid to rest. Unlike the Russians and Italians, when the Americans were outside the fence an honor guard of German soldiers accompanied them.

The American POWs, who knew the dead soldier, dressed as best they could to look like soldiers, assembled and saluted the dead soldier in the coffin as it was carried away. But, if an American soldier died trying to escape, he got nothing but a burial, buried like the Russians, without the Nazis recognizing him as a fallen soldier.

That same icy wind that bit at us while we were in line for roll call was beating on the Russian pallbearers as they escorted their dead on their final journey. They were a silent lot as they marched past, their heads hung low. As they slowly passed where I was standing, that cold wind was finding its way into barracks 18. The icy wind crawled through every nook and cranny of the poorly constructed shelter. The burlap sacks that were nailed over the open windowpanes billowed but did not stop the unwanted intruder. The uninvited guest whipped my face red as I stood, all alone, on the porch outside our barracks witnessing the procession. It was only eleven in the morning and was promising to be a long day.

For whatever reason the Germans decided to make the day worse by holding our rations until dinner. It was an appropriate day to eat part of whatever we had squirreled away from our Red Cross parcels. I had half of a D-bar left. After being on German food rations for over two months the only feeling my stomach had was empty. The hunger sensation one gets before a good hot meal, when the juices start flowing, had long since past.

When I turned to come back inside our barracks Paige Gillerman was standing by the door. "Do you think we will win the war?" Paige asked as we sat down. His speech was slower than usual.

"I think we already have."

"How's that?"

"Look around Paige, the Germans can't have much left. They don't even have enough to take care of us. They've run out of heavy equipment and are using horses to pull the trash wagon and the honey wagon."

Paige looked particularly bad that day and had lost a lot of weight since I had first met him on that transport train. Even his temples had begun to shrink into the sides of his head. He coughed, especially at night, a deep moist cough.

"What are you thinking about, Ras?" he asked. Paige always had some questions for me but I was afraid that his question might be because my expression had told him how bad I thought he looked.

"Same thing I think about every day."

"What's that?"

"Home," I said.

"What about home?" After growing up in an orphanage in Chicago, he always wanted to know something about the other soldier's "real homes."

"About playing trumpet. It always makes me feel good to think about blowing the horn. I was just thinking about out dueling my brother Harry with the trumpet. He's pretty good but I can run the chords faster than him. Being a big brother, he doesn't like it when I get to the higher notes and hold them longer than he can. Harry and I love to play the blues together, especially Clyde McCoy's *Sugar Blues*."

After a short pause Paige asked, "What's your favorite meal that your Mom cooks?"

It could be heaven or hell thinking about Mom's cooking. After avoiding the subject for the past few weeks the thought of eating home cooking changed to words real easy. Besides, I hoped that talking about Mom's cooking might help Paige feel better. Paige's expression had given away how he felt after catching the look of concern on my face seeing him in that condition.

"Pot roast, on Sunday afternoons." I answered. "We ate around four in the afternoon. Mom cooked the roast in the pressure cooker and the aroma filled the entire house. One of us boys had to peel the potatoes. Mom boiled the spuds and made mashed potatoes out of them. Harry sometimes poured milk over his potatoes before eating them. Mom also boiled carrots, cut the long way, not across like quarters. Boy, do I like cooked carrots. Taste like candy to me. Before eating, Dad said grace. Harry and I would have dived for the chow but that wasn't allowed. We had to pass each plate to the right so our sisters, Phyllis and Evelyn, got their fair share too. There were no seconds until the plate had been passed all around the table the first time. I think my Dad was afraid that Harry and I would load our plates before Phyllis and Evelyn had a chance to get their first portions. I think, maybe we even did that a couple of times, just to make 'em mad. I'll tell you something Paige, the army never fed us a meal like that."

Paige had a smile on his face as he drifted away in his private thoughts. I had forgotten how good that Sunday meal was. At home you always took it for granted that Sunday meal would be on the table.

"The pot roast was so tender," I continued now drifting off a bit on my own, "I could cut it with a fork." For the moment it felt like I was back home. "It had juicy fat on the edges and the juice squeezed out when you bit into it. I always put thick gravy Mom made from the roast drippings over the meat and butter on my potatoes, lots of creamy yellow butter. Boy, was it good. My sisters teased me because I dipped both the roast and potatoes in ketchup. The carrots were so sweet, especially after I wiped them in ketchup too. Liking ketchup runs in our family. I gotta cousin who gets ketchup in the store when we got a soda and actually drinks it while we drink our pop! Harry and I buttered our bread and used it as a sponge to soak up any gravy left on our dish. I didn't eat the crust from the bread. I don't like bread crust. I sure would eat it now. We didn't have dessert though because we were too full. Can you imagine being too full right now?"

Paige was soaking it all in. It didn't seem so cold anymore.

"Sometimes Harry and I laughed at how far our bellies stuck out after eating so much. We'd pull up our shirts and turn sideways to show everyone how big our bellies were. Mom always grinned and looked away. Our sisters made faces." I looked at Paige. The smile fixed on his face made a funny angle.

"I'm scared, Ras," he said.

"Scared of what?"

"This place, the guards."

Thought of a home cooked meal vanished as I looked into the sad eyes of a dying soldier.

"They're not going to do anything to you," I told him. "In here you just got to get by and don't worry about them."

"But they come and get some of the guys and that's the last we see of them." Rumors circulated as to what had happened to them.

"They're not going to do anything to you," I said again.

"I'm scared because I feel so weak and don't have any energy left." That was Paige's real fear.

"You look pretty good to me, Paige," I tried to be a convincing as possible. "Besides, some Red Cross parcels will be arriving soon and you'll feel as good as new after having something decent to eat. I've been saving half a D-bar. You eat it. The Red Cross can buy you dinner tonight," I said trying to lighten up the conversation a little. Paige slowly ate what remained of the chocolate bar. After sitting a few moments, Paige got up and went back to his bunk. One week later, Paige Gillerman didn't get up for roll call. Everyone knew what had happened when Paige didn't queue up to the desk to give his German serial number.

Just like the other American flyers, Paige was placed in a coffin, hoisted up on a four by four platform and carried by eight American soldiers to the cemetery. It wasn't a long way from barracks 18 to the gate leading to the cemetery but it took a long time to carry Paige outside the compound. Father Kane led prayer service and accompanied the procession as they walked away. Fifteen German guards accompanied the burying detail and fired a salute as the coffin was lowered into the grave.

Seeing Paige placed in the makeshift coffin, with the American and German dog tags hanging out of his open mouth, was a hard sight to take. Most people think that dead soldiers were tagged at the toe, but not in Stalag. The dog tags had been placed in his mouth, wedged over his front teeth, and shoved to the back of his throat.

I looked down the row of saluting soldiers, as Paige was being carried away. At the end of the line was Warren Graham, biting his lower lip and fighting back tears. Graham and Paige had become best friends. Graham was standing toe to toe with a German guard, a mean man named Sergeant Stein. Stein was bigger than Graham and had his bayonet fixed to the end of his rifle. They were staring each other down, the guard a little gleeful that an American soldier could be so hurt with the passing of his comrade. Stein was trying to provoke a confrontation. At another time and in another place, I'm certain that the farm boy would have torn the German limb from limb, but today wasn't that day. I quickly ran down to where Graham was standing. There was barely room to squeeze between the two of them, Graham pressing against the front and Stein from behind me.

"What are you thinking about, big fellow?" I asked him. Graham broke his stare with Stein and looked at me. His lower jaw protruded as he let out a sigh. Graham, like every other POW, had seen himself in that coffin.

"Come on," I said. "Let's go and say a prayer for Paige." I put my arm around Graham and led him away from the guard and over to our chapel.

15

Time for a Prayer

THE CHAPEL WASN'T THE FANCIEST IN AUSTRIA. OUR soldiers had converted a small hut into a place of worship. They had gone to great lengths to decorate it under the direction of Father Kane. A picture of a crucified Jesus Christ, painted by a French artist, hung behind the altar. Some of the POWs had traded D-bars and cigarettes with the Italian prisoners for the picture.

After Paige had been carried away, Graham and I walked into the chapel and knelt down. For a few moments neither of us said a word. Right then being in Stalag was a bit overwhelming. It was overwhelming because of our inability to change the deplorable conditions. Graham broke the silence. "If Paige had been back home, he wouldn't have died."

Before the war I came across a saying when attending church. There was a cross on the wall with Christ nailed to it. Underneath the cross, painted on the wall, was a saying "when the going gets tough, the tough get going." The Christ on the crucifix looked exactly the same as the picture we were staring at now.

Everyone has to have something to give him the inner strength to endure in tough times. The POWs in Stalag reflected on their families.

They waited to hear from them in their letters. When the POWs were growing up, they had developed hobbies and skills and now they used those hobbies to divert their attention from the conditions in Stalag. The ex-flyers had a lot to be proud of and the Germans could not rob that from them, no matter how they tried. The Americans in Stalag 17B had been selected to be flyers because of their aptitude and the fact that many of them had already attended college. The army had taught them additional specialized skills. Although we were enlisted, many of us were selected to go to on to cadet school because of our aptitude and training. We also had our faith to help us.

Faith isn't something to turn to as a last resort or just when the going got tough. I said the same prayer every night before being interned in Stalag, every night in Stalag and continued to do so the rest of my life. It was just a simple prayer thanking God for everything I had and asking that I never forget it. Those soldiers who had faith did better in Stalag. It didn't matter what denomination a soldier was; he always had more confidence when things weren't going right, even when something as depressing as rutabaga soup served for weeks on end. Most of the guys, including me, still had lots of complaints about the soup. It was, however, one more portion we had to eat before getting home so there was no reason not to thank the Good Lord before every ration, no matter how bad.

Graham and I sat a while on one of the bench seats and thought about how to deal with death and with losing a friend. I remembered asking Charlie to shoot me if I was trapped in the turret and we were going to crash. But it wasn't because I had a death wish; it was just that I wasn't going to burn underneath a crippled B-17.

"Paige had been dying for some time, Graham. You could see how much weight he had lost. He must have had pneumonia. He was getting weaker every day." I kept watching Graham as we spent the last few moments in silent prayer. Sometimes it only took one more straw on the camel's back to tip one of our soldiers over the edge. I was trying not to let it happen to Graham.

Graham wiped a tear from his eyes. "I'm okay now," he said as we got up to leave. "But I'm not going to forget about Stein."

> By: Captain Father Stephen W. Kane
> Chaplain of Stalag 17B
> Krems, Austria, 1944
>
> *Four thousand men with broken wings,*
> *Tired, wounded, crippled things*
> *We call ourselves men,*
> *And as men we try*
> *To carry on: our ideals held high*
>
> *We try to be happy*
> *We try to be gay,*
> *We know in our hearts*
> *That there will be peace some day*
>
> *We mustn't be bitter,*
> *We mustn't have fear,*
> *Tolerance, justice, love*
> *Yes, our war is so clear*
>
> *We turn to God, to renew our faith,*
> *To ask for courage to carry on*
> *As they did in the oldest volume known,*
> *Beside the waters of the Mermon*
>
> *He won't let us down wherever we be,*
> *He keeps his watch over us, for you see*
> *We are tired, wounded, crippled things,*
> *Four thousand men with broken wings*

16

Camp Life

ONE EARLY MORNING ROLL CALL WE WERE HELD IN formation longer than usual. There was confusion in the Russian compound. As we watched, the Russian soldiers were called out for their own roll call. Just like with us, if someone was missing the Germans sent their dogs into the barracks searching out the missing soldier. As we watched a Russian soldier stood up in the window with a big smile on his face. He had killed one of the German shepherds and was waving one of its legs out the window. The kriegies all got quite a hoot out of that. A few of our POWs gave the Russian some shouts of encouragement. Within minutes the guards stormed the barracks and dragged the Russian inmate across their compound and over to Commandant Kuhn's quarters. A few minutes later, three shots rang out. Everyone went silent. One of the guards, Sergeant Struck said, "The culprit has been done away with." When it came to killing Russian soldiers the Germans had little remorse.

A number of us had attended different classes during the day, learning a foreign language or studying history, law or economics. Classes were taught by fellow POWs to help fill the time. There were even classes on playing cards including pinochle and poker. Bridge class had the best attendance.

Teamwork and camaraderie were strong among the American POWs in Stalag 17B. We had a common enemy. The POWs prayed together with Father Kane. All of us lived in the same miserable conditions.

All the camaraderie came to a temporary end with the camp bridge championship. Barracks 14 played against 36, barracks 19 against 39 and so on. Bridge was by far the most interesting game played in Stalag and it wasn't long after the card decks were drawn and classes were held that a league was formed. Each of the barracks determined who were the best, or luckiest players. William Ghiz, a great guy from Massachusetts, and one hell of a card player, was my partner. Through a process of elimination the championship was won. There were forty teams from our barracks alone. The team that won their barracks went on to the camp championship.

"Three hearts," our competition bid. Bill and I were in the championship round of barracks 18. Both teams were vulnerable and neither team had any points. The next team scoring one hundred points won. We were playing with the original deck of cards I had made out of paper, torn from the Red Cross parcels.

"Three spades," Bill responded.

"Three no trump." Bill was over bid. If our opponents won the hand, they would win the barracks' championship.

I studied the soldier across from me. "Four spades," I responded.

Bill and I won the honor to represent barracks 18. I was "lucky" partly because I could tell every one of the cards in the original deck from the back as well as the front.

The camp quarterfinal round was on. There were only eight teams left. Betting was at a fever pitch. The bookies were hard at work. Treasures were on the line: D-bars, raisins, prunes, coffee, cigarettes. Rules were agreed on.

"Anyone caught signaling loses the hand, not vulnerable three hundred points to the other side, cheating when your team is vulnerable, five hundred points," announced the appointed sergeant at arms in charge of rules. Each team had its own vigilante group to watch the competition. These were the same GIs who served on secret committees with you where one mishap could mean your death. Now they were across the table, arms folded and staring at you.

"Anyone looking up, coughing, clearing his throat or any other unusual move constitutes signaling," the sergeant said. "You must play the cards with your right hand and hold them in your left. An impartial observer from a non-involved barracks will settle any disagreement." In order to win, you had to give yourself an advantage and you had to be good at it. Bill and I were very good. We had been playing in the tournament for four weeks and easily won the next round.

"It's the semifinal match today and we've got a whole Red Cross parcel waged on you guys," one of the kriegies from barracks 18 said.

Bill and I sat across the table from two former tail gunners from barracks 33.

It would have been a great ending to the story if we had wound up as camp champs, able to capture most of the loot as a reward for ourselves and our buddies, but that wasn't in the cards. We were knocked off in the semifinal match. The one great reward was that we used up dull time and provided entertainment for ourselves plus a vast number of our fellow kriegies, some of whom got "rich" along the way.

Our soldiers were always trying to get the best of the Germans in some way. One was to have contact with the outside world. Uncensored contact with the outside world was strictly regulated by the Naxis. Except for the occasional visit by the Red Cross representative, we were isolated. Radio receivers were strictly forbidden and were the cause of many barracks being searched. But the Germans had to deal with the fact that the captured American flyers included radio operators and repairmen. Some of the POWs had the expertise to construct receivers. Bert Steiler was just such an operator and repairman.

"We need a tuning coil and an earphone or it'll never work," Steiler told us. One man's junk was another's treasure, especially in Stalag. A

German guard had discarded a tooth powder cylinder in the trash house, a rusty, one-half inch tube, perfect for a tuning coil.

The headset was another matter. The Italian POWs had headsets. Bargaining for one of them started at a high price. It cost several unopened Red Cross parcels and most of our supply of cigarettes to get one with a single earpiece.

"We need to have some wire to wrap the tube," Steiler said. The barracks had plenty of electrical cord connected to nonworking lights. All we had to do was rip about twenty feet of the cord out of the walls and strip the wire out of the cord. The tube was attached to a box in case it had to be concealed in fast order.

The top of the cylinder was buffed bare. Bert wrapped the tube with one hundred twenty turns of the wire. One end was conected to a ground. Off the wire leading to the ground, another wire was brought back to the headset.

We made an antenna out of another piece of electrical cord. Then it was back to the trash house to get a discarded light bulb. On the base of the light bulb was a strip of brass. Bert connected the free end of the tuner to the strip of brass which was in turn connected with a piece of wire to the antenna. Off the wire leading to the antenna another wire was connected to the headset.

The British Broadcasting Corporation directed a very strong radio beam over the continent. On some days it made our receiver work like a charm. When we got the receiver in working order, the BBC was broadcasting a music program. Bert got to listen first.

"I don't believe my ears," he exclaimed when we first got it working. "They're playing *Don't Fence Me In!*"

None of us thought it was meant for us but it sure did make us sit up and think about our imprisonment. Soon, other receivers were made. The ex-flyers listened for the progress of our troops and hoped for an early end to the war. Everyone passed on the information to the camp "news center." From there it went for distribution to each of the barracks, at the end of mail call, by an American POW who served as the camp postman.

17

The Ninth Life

THERE WASN'T ANYTHING PARTICULARLY DIFFERENT ABOUT March 3, 1944, not until evening began to set in. The day had been very unexciting. Between rain earlier in the day and melting snow piled up around the camp, the ground was too wet and too muddy for any outdoor sports. The nights held a hint that they were getting a bit warmer as winter's grip was beginning to loosen.

The sun had just fallen below the horizon and we were due for our bowl of potato soup for the fifth day in a row. Only McDowell and Graham were still outside. They had been hanging around the fence looking at the cemetery. Suddenly Graham broke into the barracks, looking very excited and out of breath.

"You guys got to come quick. Mac's spotted a cat wandering around outside the fence!" he said in a loud whisper so as not to alert the entire barracks.

Charlie, Steiler, Graham, Phelper, Ghiz, four more of the other guys and myself slipped out or the barracks and scurried behind barracks 19 and 20 down to the fence. The German guard tower was no more than fifty feet away. Three of the guards eyed us suspiciously.

Outside the barbed wire fence, a mangy, stray black cat had caught the scent of a rodent and was perched, staring, head nodding, near some bent over grass, ready to spring whenever the rodent surfaced. The patch of grass must have been about a foot tall when the snow caught it several months earlier. Now it was gray, dead grass, wedged between the melting snow and some mud. The chipmunk, or whatever was the intended prey, had run into a hole below the patch of grass.

"If kitty comes in through the fence," Graham said. "We'll have feline steak for dinner. Forget Jerry's rotten potato soup tonight." My eyebrows went up as I sized up the other boys. Anything sounded better than another bowl of the same soup. After three months of enduring a starvation diet the thought of meat of any kind had us licking our chops.

"Look," McDowell said. "We need a plan. Steiler and me will go down this side of the fence a few paces. Charlie, you and Graham go up that way." McDowell was pointing up the fence toward the guard tower. "The rest of you get back from the fence and spread out. If Pussy Willow here comes through the fence then the four of us will block her escape. You guys form a circle and close in on her as fast as possible. We'll only get one crack at her so don't blow it."

Two new guards joined the ones already in the tower. They didn't have a clue as to what we were up to. There were five of them now, all standing there holding their rifles and being very vigilant but not interfering. Any time the POWs went by the fence the guards thought the prisoners were going to make a run for it.

We spread out and waited. Nothing appeared out of the hole that caught the cat's attention. Within ten minutes the cat's head started to bob up and down as if its prey was going to appear, then she just lost interest in the hunt. Almost as if she was attracted to the camp and with no sense of concern, she walked under the fence and picked her way around the cans piled under the warning wire and right into the ambush. When she was twenty feet inside the warning wire Charlie, Graham, McDowell and Steiler cut off her escape route.

"Now!" Steiler shouted.

The circle closed. The cat bolted back in an attempt to get out through the fence and in so doing ran right into Graham who jumped on top of her. His landing crushed the cat, but just to be sure he twisted its head in a circle. Graham was covered with mud when he stood up.

"Look at this prize catch!" Graham exclaimed holding the animal up by the back of the neck. Its eyes were still wide open and its head was hanging down. "Pussy Willow here just lived her ninth life."

"Now what are we going to do with it?" Charlie asked.

"Skin it and eat it," Graham answered.

He carried the dead cat back to barracks 18 where it caused quite a commotion. Graham used the top of a tin can to cut the hide. The skin peeled off surprisingly easy. Butchering it was another story. I couldn't believe how bad it smelled when Graham gutted it. I almost vomited. The rest of the guys in the barracks got a little testy and made us finish the job outside. We managed to get meat off the chest, along the spine, butt and back legs: ten small pieces of raw feline steak, each no bigger than an inch square. The only problem was that there were eleven of us. After finishing, we went back into the barracks to clean up and wash our dinner. It was almost nine o'clock and it would be time for the lights to be out very soon.

"Anybody not want their piece?" Graham asked.

"Not after that little escapade," McDowell answered.

"How about we draw straws, short straw loses," Steiler suggested.

No one liked that suggestion either, so being a gambling man, I suggested, "Let's cut cards for it, low man looses." No one liked that idea either, seems I had been winning too many card games.

"Okay," McDowell said. "Get our forks. Evenly distribute the ten pieces in the middle of the table. One of the other guys in the barracks can hit the light and then turn it back on in a few seconds. It will be pitch black in the barracks with the light out. When it's out, we'll all jab for a piece. One guy loses out. If someone gets more than one piece you got to give one back, your choice of which one. If there are any pieces left on the table no one can jab for a piece with the light on. For those who didn't get a piece the process starts all over for the remaining guys who don't have a piece until only one guy is left without one. Fair enough?"

It sounded fair enough. Ten out of eleven chances to get a share by skewering one of them was a chance I could live with any day. By now everyone in our end of the barracks had gathered around, over a hundred and twenty other POWs watching the happenings.

"Everyone get their fork. At the signal one of you guys," McDowell pointed toward the crowd that had gathered, "kill the light and in a few seconds screw it back in."

"Wait a minute," Charlie chimed in. "Aren't we going to boil it?" For the moment, no one said anything; we just stood there with our forks in hand looking the small pieces of feline tartare on the table. I for one was thinking of how bad it smelled when we gutted it.

"Better not," Ben said. "The meat will shrink and lose its nutrients. We'll eat it raw. Now everybody get ready. Steiler, you say when." We each eyed the biggest piece closest to us that we thought no one else would jab at.

"Now!" Steiler shouted and the room went pitch black.

"Ahhhh!" Graham shrieked just after the light was cut. The light came back on. Graham was holding on to biggest piece of meat but there were three forks stuck in the back of his hand!

"What were you doing, Warren?" I asked him. The room had gone silent.

"Just thought it was a faster way to get the meat if I grabbed for it." He had let go of his bounty and was rubbing the back of his bleeding hand. Fortunately none of the bones were broken. Graham was his usual unflappable self.

"Looks like it was," I said shaking my head.

The ten pieces were then divided between everyone but Graham, but each of us decided to give him a portion of ours. No one cared what piece they ended up with. While chewing on our prize, we told the rest of the guys in the barracks the entire story. Everyone had a good time even if they hadn't dined like we had. Truth is, that little piece of raw cat tasted pretty good.

When I turned in, I was still in disbelief about what Warren had done. Graham's bunk was across from mine. "Hey Graham," I said after everyone had settled in. The light was out and the barracks was otherwise silent.

"Yo."

"Your hand okay?"

"Yeah, it's all right."

"But it's gotta be hurting."

"Hurts a little."

"Graham," I said again, after a few minutes had passed.

"Yo."

"Don't do anything like that again."

"I won't! Huh, huh, huh, huh."

18

The Escape Committee

ON APRIL 10, 1944, AFTER SPENDING FOUR MONTHS IN captivity, most of it in Stalag 17B, I was tired of roll call and the way guards tired to make us conform to their demands. Roll call was at six-thirty this particular morning and we were supposed to queue up to a table in the middle of the yard for identification. After getting up to the table we were instructed to give our name, rank and our German dog tag number. It took an hour moving at a snail's pace to get to the table where the German guards were conducting the check.

"Next."

"William E. Rasmussen, Staff Sergeant, USAF, POW number, um, I forgot."

The way the guards had of correcting this was to send the POW to the back of the line, not just for his barracks but also for the entire American section. By the time I made it back to the desk I knew my German serial number, 100483 and never pretended to forget it again.

All 4,200 captured American flyers who ended up in Stalag 17B had one thing in mind: escape. It was a dream that kept our hopes alive; get out of Stalag and return to fight the Nazis again. To the American GIs, escape meant that they had bested the Germans and that Stalag and all the regulations had meant nothing. In actuality, planning an escape was as much an escape from the boredom we faced as it was a dream to keep our hopes alive.

For most of us, the only way to fly again was to get out, and that wasn't likely to happen. It wasn't until I got involved in planning an escape from the German prison camp that the reality of never being inside a B-17 again set in. A lot of the ex-flyers were having a hard time coping in POW camp because they knew they were trapped. Their flying days were over. They had gone from being an American flyer to being a prisoner of war. The reality was that the POWs weren't going to get home, let alone fly, unless the Allies won the war and the Germans didn't kill us in the meantime. Our best hope for the present time was to stay alive. Recognizing that was one of the reasons I got tagged to be chairman of the escape committee of Stalag 17B.

The captured aircraft engineers, mechanics, hydraulic, electrical and tire specialists all thought they could build a plane and fly out. Someone always had an idea on how to make it happen and was more than happy to share his plans with the rest of us. Escaping via an aircraft was a noble idea but one that was not about to happen. First, there were no materials to build an aircraft; second, there was no fuel. How could an aircraft be hidden from the Germans? Yet, every flyboy loved to talk about it. "If we could just get this engine part, or that fuselage piece, we'd be on our way," was the camp talk.

The first real attempt to escape from Stalag 17B was made before I arrived by some soldiers in the "old part" of the camp, section eight, barracks 33. The Germans had given the prisoners some whitewash to paint the outside of their buildings. In fact, once the Germans saw how good the first building looked, they ordered every one of the barracks to be painted white. But two of the prisoners hid some away and used the whitewash to camouflage themselves and their clothing. Plans were made and two flyers picked to make the break. At night, under cover of a heavy snowstorm, the two soldiers who were prepped to escape slid under the warning wire and approached the fence. Everything went as planned until both of them were past the warning wire. Then the lights from two of the towers suddenly focused on them. It was as if the guards knew where and when the escape was to take place.

Both soldiers threw up their hands to surrender, but the guards machined gunned both of them where they stood. One died and the other was wounded in the leg. The German guards walked up to him and shot him again, then turned around and riddled barracks 20 with machine gun fire, seriously injuring another POW lying in his bunk. The Germans did not allow other American POWs to bring in the dead soldier or allow anyone to go near the wounded soldier. Several hours passed before permission was granted to give him medical attention.

"After the machine gun fire the only thing that broke the silence was the coarse, wet breathing of the first soldier before he died," one of the ex-flyers who was in the camp at the time told me. "No one did anything because there wasn't anything we could do."

Kenneth Kurtenbach had been elected to be our MOC (Man of Confidence). He was a rugged looking guy and very deliberate with his words. All of us thought his most important responsibility was to register protests about the conditions in Stalag with the German Commandant. If the protests fell on deaf ears, he lodged the same complaint to the Swiss when they inspected the camp. As it turned out, Ken had other responsibilities. It was on April 10 that word was passed for me to attend an afternoon meeting in barracks 37 and not to discuss it with any of the other soldiers. Two large ex-flyers, with stern looks on their faces met me at the door. One of them just nodded his head, motioning for me to go inside. I wasn't sure what was going on; I was kind of hoping it was a large stakes poker game. Funny thing was that no one had told me to bring any of the cigarettes I had won and had stashed away to use as currency. Instead, Kurtenbach and two other GIs whom I did not know were sitting at a table. Several others were behind them in the shadows.

"Sit down, Ras," Kurtenbach said as I surveyed the situation.

I turned the chair around before sitting down, so that there was no back of the chair to block a quick escape, then put my arms around the back of the chair and rocked forward as I looked around. By the looks on their faces, something was up and it did not look good. Not sure what was going on, I was feeling instinctively cautious.

"We're going to offer you a job and it's an offer we think you should take," Kurtenbach said.

"Does it pay well?" I kept the conversation as loose as possible.

"It's non-paying."

I nodded at his answer. "Are the hours long?" I was still trying to size up what they were getting at.

"It's a 24-7 job," he answered.

"Nothing like staying busy in this hell hole," I said. "Who'll I be working with?"

"We'll let you know who you'll get involved with. For right now, it's just us. Let's just say you're replacing someone who's no longer with us," Kurtenbach said. "It seems he wore out his welcome with the Krauts."

I just sat there and didn't reply. I was trying to get a read on Kurtenbach's face. Obviously Kurtenbach wanted me for something that the Germans didn't want done and the last guy that had the job was no longer with us.

"Okay, I'm interested, but you've got to tell me more than that."

"Someone needs to coordinate the escape plans for the camp. No one tries to get out again unless the escape committee that you head up approves. Anyone disappears from the camp, all the information about how it was planned and who helped him filters back through you. We already have a man in every barracks watching what's going on. No one tries to escape unless it's approved by the escape committee first."

I just sat there in silence. Every POW wanted out of this place and the Germans knew that escape organizations existed. The rules were that you got shot trying to escape, not planning to escape, at least those were the posted rules.

"I'll help," was my answer. I'd do anything to get back at the Germans.

"There's a code of silence," Kurtenbach said. "You relate your information only to this committee and only with me present. Turns out that one of our men is actually a plant, and has an inside path on what's going down. Somehow he knows pretty much everything that we are doing." Then everything Kurtenbach was saying came together. A network already established in Stalag was trying to devise methods of escape. None of them were working. The Germans had planted a mole who was divulging our escape plans. He was also trying to identify the ex-flyers who might know something special about the pipeline of B-17 bombers. Those soldiers had been taken away by the Germans for interrogation. They never came back. Ostensibly the ex-flyer who headed the escape committee disappeared because they knew something that the Germans considered vital to their war effort. The mole was a trusted GI whose identity we were going to have to discover.

I left barracks 37 and wandered aimlessly back to barracks 18 thinking about what Kurtenbach had said.

The next day, while I was sitting on our front deck, passing the time and thinking about escaping, Charlie walked by.

"What are you doing?" Charlie asked me.

"Counting to 16,064,955."

"What are you doing that for? That number mean something to you?"

"Yeah, my serial number on my dog tags, 16064955."

"You got to be kidding me. How long do you think that will take?" Charlie had that familiar smile on his face.

"I've got that all figured out, Charlie. If I count by hundreds, one number every two seconds on average, it will take me just over one hundred seventy-eight hours. At two hours a day, I'll be done at the beginning of next year!"

"Gee Ras, that's one way to stay busy, but I think I'll pass on it." Charlie walked away shaking his head. I finished the count in less than a year.

Soon after the meeting with Kurtenbach, the first new idea for an escape was hatched. It came from Bill Gibson who had devised his own novel way of getting out of the camp. "When they come to clean out the garbage hut, bury me under the trash," he said. "When the truck is well outside of Stalag, I'll just jump out and make my way to England. I'll send all of you a post card from home." The committee approved the plan with very little debate.

The next time the trash wagon came to take away the garbage, Gibson crawled in. Some of the kriegies shoveled the back full of rubbish until it was piled high enough that no one could see him. We watched as the horse drawn trash wagon slowly pulled away. When the trash wagon neared the gate, Gibson couldn't stand the stench any longer. He jumped up and gave himself over to the guards. His little dash for home landed him a couple of days in solitary confinement.

Several other escape attempts were made. The most detailed and time consuming was digging tunnels under the perimeter of the compound. One of the POWs just voiced the idea when we were sitting around. "Bet we could dig our way out," he said. It seemed harmless enough. It certainly occupied a lot of time. The committee approved the plan. Barracks 20 in section five and barracks 40 in section nine were closest to the perimeter, just inside the fence that separated the compound from the cemetery. The committee elected to have the first tunnel dug from barracks 40. The plan was to remove the floorboards below the hearth and dig east towards the cemetery. To dig, the ex-flyers used utensils made out of the empty cans. The sides of the tunnel were braced with wood from the Red Cross parcel crates as well as some stolen fence pieces.

Each day POWs carried sand in their pockets out of the barracks and spread it in the yard. But neither tunnel was ever completed.

No one escaped from Stalag.

19

A German Mole

AFTER THAT FIRST MEETING WITH KURTENBACH, I STROLLED over to the camp bulletin board where the guards posted certain news clippings they wanted us to read. On my way back to barracks 18, I spotted Charlie on the porch.

"Being in here and not knowing what they have in mind for us is starting to get to me," Charlie said.

"Well," I told him, "you don't have to fret about it anymore, Charlie. There's a Berlin newspaper article posted on the bulletin board that says Hitler's 'got some special plans for all the interned enemy flyers who caused the destruction of their people, cities and factories.' Apparently the American flyers have been doing a good job of bringing the conflict to an end and Hitler's upset about it. Funny thing is the story didn't mention anything about his part in the war."

"Do you think he means it, Ras?"

"Oh yeah, I reckon he's got a lot of plans for us." I let it go at that, and walked into the barracks and thought about a way to catch the German mole. Kurtenbach, the representatives from four of the other barracks, including barracks 40 and 20, and three of Kurtenbach's inner circle met again just before the Germans caved in the first tunnel. It was May 10, 1944.

"Look," I explained to Kurtenbach and the other committee members at the meeting, "The Germans didn't plant a mole in the camp to tell them about our escape attempts. They know that we're trying to find ways to get out of here. We're certainly not flying out, so we've got to get out underground. Besides, you all know that if anyone escapes, it's going to be a miracle if they can make it to the resistance and back to England. It's much more likely that they'll get shot, just like the last two guys who tried to escape. Our crew couldn't get back to England after being shot down near the Belgium border. We had foreign currency, rations, maps, a compass and a lot less distance to travel. Stalag's in eastern Austria and even farther from a safe haven."

No one said anything as I waited a few moments to make my other points. They all knew the truth about trying to escape but didn't want to admit it and get robbed of what hope they had of getting out. "For the Germans, digging tunnels is a way for the energetic POWs to stay busy while they keep an eye on us. I'll bet any one of you here, your next Red Cross parcel, that they know that we are digging a tunnel right now. They're just waiting for the right time to cave it in, or shoot the first one of us that crawls out of it."

"It makes sense," one of the soldiers said. "Besides, with the number of roll calls we have to go through, it wouldn't be long before they know who's missing. They'll be right after whoever did make it out. How do you think they do it?"

"Besides someone telling them? They probably have microphones that monitor the activity, especially near the perimeter," I said. "I'll tell you what they're after and why they had someone infiltrate the camp. There's lots of valuable information that 4,200 American flyers know. It's a lot more valuable to them than a few POWs making a run for it. I'll tell you something else. They're getting good information or they wouldn't be going through all the effort of having a spy in here. He might as well be in the officers' Stalag. There are lots of things the POWs talk about in here besides escape. In fact, some of them talk too much. The mole hears them and reports what he's heard. I've heard some talk about our radar system and ammunition factories and about some other key installations in England that are in reach of the German bombers. It's stuff that POWs need to keep quiet about because the Germans have a pair of ears in the camp."

"If we find him, I'm going to kill him," another one of the soldiers declared. It made him mad just thinking about the German spy. The rest of us stared at him for a second. No one had talked about what we would do if we did find him. The penalty, if any of us were caught spying, was death.

"It certainly will give us a new problem, what to do with him if we discover his identity," I added. "We'll cross that bridge when we get to it."

"I'll tell you something else that I know first-hand: the mole also wants the information their interrogation officer, that Major Rolfing, was asking me about at Federal prison."

"We heard about your encounter with Rolfing," Kurtenbach said. "Seems Rolfing didn't think much of you, had you stay a night out in the cold."

"The feeling was mutual," I replied, realizing that there must be a number of our soldiers who reported to Kurtenbach about the other POWs, including me. It made me feel a little better about our organizational network.

"Look," I went on, "McDowell told me that Rolfing had a book entitled The 91st Bomb Group. Rolfing knew the answers to all the questions he asked me. What he was trying to do was to see how much the flyers would talk. He was trying to find someone who would give him a clue as to how the 17s got on the runway at Bassingbourn and the other bases in England. Then the German bombers could try to take them out before the 17s ever had a chance to fly bombing missions over Europe. That's one of the key reasons why the spy is here, trying to finish Rolfing's job."

"That doesn't leave us with many options," Kurtenbach said. "We can't let him have a free rein of the place."

"The thing we have to realize is that the chances of us surviving to the end of the war in here are a lot better than the odds of getting out, like it or not. That may not be what you want to hear but that's reality. We've got to be careful that no one gets too ambitious about escape plans. Believe me, I'm not against trying, as long as we're careful. In the meantime, we lay a trap and catch the mole."

"How?" Kurtenbach asked.

"I've been thinking about a trap. Let's call it an information maze. A good place to start is to consider everyone who knew the escape plans about the two POWs who were shot trying to escape. The guards had to know about their plan because they put them in the lights, just at the right time. Everyone who knows about the tunnel being dug from barracks 40 needs to be put on another list. If they discover the tunnel, the mole must be someone on both lists, and we narrow down the number of suspects. Then we leak some new information that we don't want the Krauts to know, like the existence of a radio, to POWs on a third list. Once the guards have the radio, the mole's inside the maze, he's on all three lists. There's just one thing we need to realize. In order to catch him, some valuable property is going to be lost. We've got to be careful not to lose any of our soldiers along the way. Digging escape tunnels could go a long way to help find this guy. Like I said, it might even be for the best if the tunnels are never used. Besides, our guys keep busy, and what better way is there to catch a mole than digging a tunnel?"

So the plan was hatched. No one outside the escape committee knew. The chief of barracks 40 was told to keep the tunnel "top secret," which meant that only a few hundred POWs knew about it. The tunnel was anything but "top secret," but at least it was a start.

Just three days after the meeting a German truck was seen inside the perimeter of the American section. "What's that truck doing?" one of the kriegies asked. The POWs stopped mulling about in the yard, and eyed the truck. Heavy equipment was rarely seen inside the perimeter. When the heavy truck drove over the tunnel between barracks 40 and the fence, the tunnel caved in. Luckily, no one was inside digging when it happened. The list of kriegies who knew about the escape plans of the ex-flyers who had been shot trying to escape was matched with those who knew about the tunnel from barracks 40. The information maze was funneling down.

Then we used a radio that some of the ex-flyers had bartered for, trading cigarettes with the Italians. The radio was passed on to select groups of POWs in different barracks. They listened to the BBC and passed the news throughout the camp. The Germans came a few days later and confiscated it. We cross-referenced the lists. The number of possible suspects was getting smaller.

In the meantime, there was talk in the camp about one of the soldiers being the informant. One of the POWs had an accent and was nicknamed "Abby the Mole." He stuck out like a sore thumb and the buzz around the barracks was to avoid him. "Hey Abby," the kriegies shouted as he came near. Everyone knew he was around so he couldn't overhear anything. After a while we figured Abby was just a decoy for the real mole, who was much more of a chameleon blending in as American flyer. The commandant soon ordered Abby out of camp and assigned him guard duty.

With all that was happening, some of the POWs became a little anxious and wrongly accused one of their fellow GIs of being a spy without good evidence. A certain amount of this behavior had to be overlooked, so as not to tip off the real mole. If he suspected we were getting close to discovering his real identity, then the commandant would pluck him out.

Each flyer who remained in the maze was being investigated. Kurtenbach assigned a number of his confidants to discretely talk to the soldiers still being investigated about their background; where they were from, what bombardment group they flew with when they arrived at Stalag, and so forth. As it turned out, a POW from Cleveland, named Pearce, had arrived at Stalag 17B at the same time the other POWs were transferred from Stalag 7. No one else in camp had flown with him. No one was aware of him being in Federal prison or at Dulag Luft.

While digging the second tunnel from barracks 20, our break came. "Okay," Kurtenbach said at the next meeting, "Pass the information on to Pearce about the new tunnel. Let's close the trap." Sure enough, two days later the honey wagon pulled up in front of barracks 20 and pumped the tunnel full of raw sewage. Once again, it was a good thing not to be in the tunnel when the Germans decided to fill it in. The decision was made to confront Pearce about his activities during daylight hours when the guards would not be concerned about a group of POWs getting together.

The POWs in barracks 37 were told to leave because of a secret meeting. The committee members were there along with a few of the other POWs. I took Graham with me. Pearce was lured into the barracks. He had no more sat down when one of the Kurtenbach's men grabbed him from the back.

"How did the Krauts find out the location of the two tunnels, Pearce?" Kurtenbach shouted at him. "You knew about both of them!"

"How come right after you were told about the radio the guards came and got it?" another POW demanded to know.

"Pearce, you knew about the two soldiers who were white washed and tried to escape. In fact, you approved of the plan," Kurtenbach added.

After more intense interrogation Pearce admitted to being the spy. "Yeah, I'm German. I spent a good deal of time in the States and came back to help our cause, so what that you discovered my identity. I'll be out of here in no time." He had a smirk on his face. Without hesitation, one of our soldiers grabbed him from behind and snapped his neck.

"Jesus, now what are we going to do?" Graham asked. "This could be a real trouble."

"We've got to hide him where the guards can't find him or we'll all be shot!" Kurtenbach said.

After a moment of silence Graham said, "Bury him in the 24-holer." It sounded like it might work.

Two of you go to the latrine and keep anyone from using it until we can get Pearce's body over there and shove it down," Kurtenbach said. "Tell them to use the can in their own barracks for the next hour."

Pearce's body was placed in the middle of the group of POWs and carried to the 24-holer as if he was walking. We stuffed his body down. A few minutes later it floated to the surface.

"Can you believe it?" Graham shouted. "He floats! Huh, huh, huh, huh. Someone's gonna have to keep shovin him down. Eventually his body will decompose. After that it won't float." Another secret committee was formed.

"Where's Sergeant Pearce?" The guards asked the next morning at roll call.

"He crawled out of here!" shouted one of the kriegies.

"Yeah, he and some of the others made it out of here last night," came another answer.

"Expect I'll get a card from him soon," said another.

The soldiers on the "burial committee" went to the latrine at regular intervals. They kept everyone else out while they took wooded planks and shoved the corpse back down in the raw sewage. It took the better part of a month before the body would no longer float. The smell of the latrine, at its worse in the summer months, masked the putrid smell of the decomposing body. None of our GIs got singled out for interrogation again and the Germans lost their source for valuable information.

The ex-flyers had won a samll battle against the Nazis.

WRITE VERY CLEARLY WITHIN THE LINES. IN ORDER TO EXPEDITE CENSORSHIP, LETTERS SHOULD BE TYPED OR PRINTED IN BLOCK CAPITALS.

Mar. 18, 1945

Dear Bro. Boy what Leland hasn,T been doing the past two weeks!!! Mar. 1,2,3 (District tournaments at Traverse) my class spent at the Park Place. We decided we would get rid of a little surplus Dough and really take things easy. We not only Did that but we won the tournament too. Sooooo the following week found "Yours truly" in Petoskey to help lead our team to Victory. Pretty good leading too 'cause we won there also. This last Thursday we met a team a trifle too stiff as we were froze out in the state semi finals. Well, I Play for dances regularly on Saturday nights and once in awhile other times. I'm still giving piano lessons also. I hear from Keith and Cub regularly and mom hears from Mrs. Quim p quite often. Spring is a little early this year. The ice and snow are pretty well gone and the tulips and daffodils are poking their heads through. This morning I picked up Topper's winter collection of bones which amounted to half a cow. I have one of my Senior pictures on your dresser. Our invitations came Friday and I'm adding one of those to your collection upstairs. Graduation is slated

TOP PANEL

for May 29. I hope you can make it. I took scholarship exams for U of M last Wednesday. They were pretty stiff but I hope I make it. I'm making a new suit for Easter. Pretty neat. I'm making it as a 4-H member with the help of our Home-Ec Teacher. Just enough space for an appropriate ending of - So long with love - Phil.

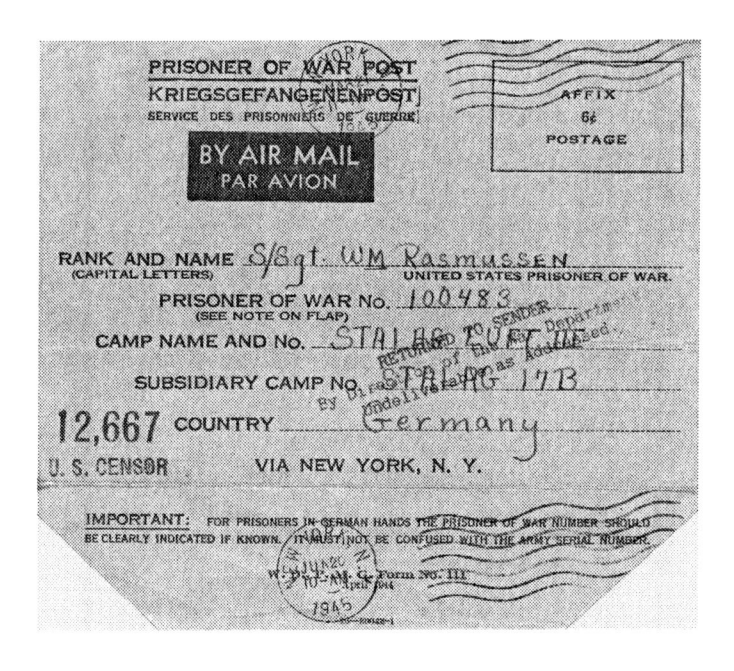

PRISONER OF WAR POST
KRIEGSGEFANGENENPOST
SERVICE DES PRISONNIERS DE GUERRE

BY AIR MAIL
PAR AVION

RANK AND NAME S/Sgt. WM Rasmussen
(CAPITAL LETTERS)   UNITED STATES PRISONER OF WAR.
PRISONER OF WAR No. 100483
CAMP NAME AND No. STALAG LUFT III
SUBSIDIARY CAMP No. STALAG 17B
12,667 COUNTRY Germany
U.S. CENSOR   VIA NEW YORK, N.Y.

Letters sent to German POW camps identified the American GI by his German POW number, not his American serial number. This letter, postmarked June 1945, was sent from Rasmussen's sister, Phyllis, but was undelivered and returned to sender. Before it could arrive the Russians had bombed Stalag 17B.

> **Kriegsgefangenenlager** Datum: Sept. 11, 44
>
> Dear Don, Bid & Kids: I received your very welcome letter Sept 5th & am hoping that I am fortunate in receiving more — So far I have heard from my folks & you. I hope you have received my cards — I wrote in March & April. Cub is @ home according to your letter give him my best & tell him to write. My love to all — Write soon, Bill

Rasmussen's friends, the Scamehorns, saved two of his letters that were sent to them from Stalag 17B and returned them after the war. This letter was written September 11, 1944.

On April 5, 1945, 4,200 captured American flyers filed out of Stalag 17B, in rows of three, on a forced march across Austria. (photograph by Ben H. Phelper)

One of the causalities of the forced march. A soldier lay dead, dehydrated from dysentery and lack of proper provisions. (photograph by Ben H. Phelper)

POWs on the forced march developed blistered feet with open sores. Soaking them in a cold creek felt good, if only for a short time. (photograph by Ben H. Phelper)

The forced march ended in at the juncture of the Inn and Salzach Rivers. Several of the POWs worked their way to a bluff overlooking the Inn River where they could see American tanks traveling east. (photograph by Ben H. Phelper)

The twenty-two day forced march across northern Austria started near Krems and ended in the Leach Forest outside of Braunau.

The crew of the *Hell's Belle*. The photo was taken at a reunion in September 1988. Pictured left to right are Gerald McDowell, Bert Stieler, Bill Rasmussen, Cecil Comer, Charles Dyer, and Charles Quinn.

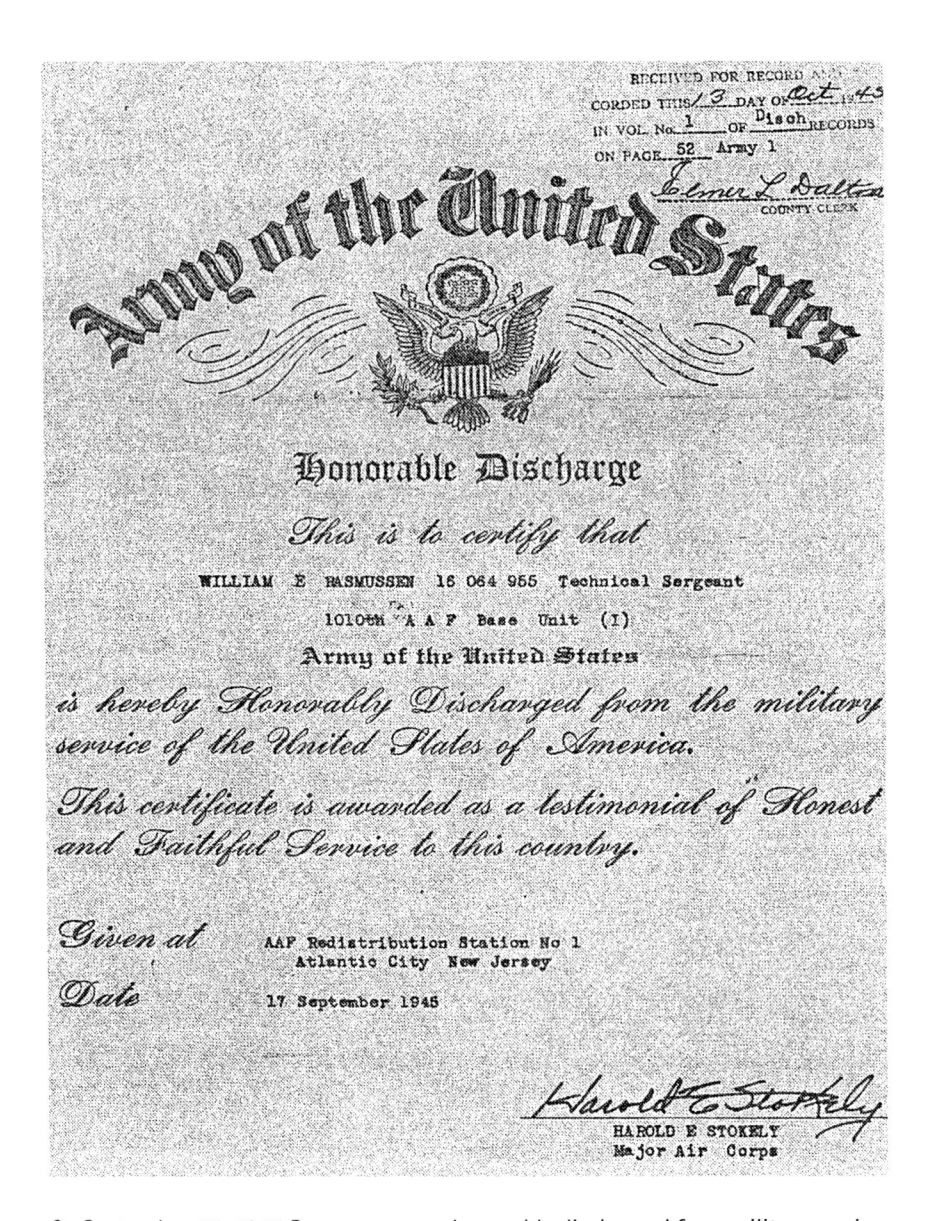

Army of the United States

Honorable Discharge

This is to certify that

WILLIAM E RASMUSSEN 16 064 955 Technical Sergeant
1010th A A F Base Unit (I)
Army of the United States

is hereby Honorably Discharged from the military service of the United States of America.

This certificate is awarded as a testimonial of Honest and Faithful Service to this country.

Given at AAF Redistribution Station No 1
Atlantic City New Jersey

Date 17 September 1945

HAROLD E STOKELY
Major Air Corps

On September 17, 1945 Rasmussen was honorably discharged from military service.

> The United States of America
> honors the memory of
> William E. Rasmussen
>
> This certificate is awarded by a grateful nation in recognition of devoted and selfless consecration to the service of our country in the Armed Forces of the United States.
>
> *William J. Clinton*
> President of the United States

After his passing, the President of the United States issued a certificate in the memory of William E. Rasmussen. It recognized Rasmussen's devotion and dedication to America through his service in the armed forces.

20

Mail Call

ON JUNE 5, 1944, SUMMER HAD ARRIVED AND WITH IT, A warm rain. It was midday and a number of the ex-flyers stood outside their respective barracks naked, lathered up and waiting for the rainwater to run off their barrack's roof and rinse them off. There had already been one roll call for our barracks at five-thirty this morning and another one had been ordered. The guards liked to have extra roll calls, especially if the weather was bad. But I had decided that the early morning's roll call was my last one for the day. I had enjoyed the warm rain and feeling clean and wasn't going to stand in line waiting for my name to be called out a second time. Today, I was going to lie in my sack and listen to the rain beat on our roof and fill the tin cans that hung from the ceiling. Today, I was not going to answer the second roll call.

    Everyone who wasn't already outside taking a shower, filed out of barracks 18. I climbed to the back of the top bunk and hid. The rain fell and the guards counted two hundred forty-one POWs, one missing. They counted again and had everyone queued up through the mud to the table in the middle of the yard where the guards identified the prisoners one by one by their serial number.

"Sergeant Rasmussen not accounted for," the guard announced.

At any other time making two hundred POWs stand out in the rain got the hair on their collective backs up, but not this time because it meant keeping the guards outside and frustrated because one was missing. The only problem was that they sent their hungry German shepherd and Doberman pinschers through the barracks. I silently hid in the top bunk and the dogs didn't find me. Then, in came the guards, nosing into every potential hiding place until one of them came to my bunk. His hands came over the top bunk and he hoisted himself up.

"BOOOO!" I yelled at the top of my voice, just as his nose came into view. He fell backward right on his butt. I practically fell out of the bed laughing until two more guards showed up and dragged me out of the bunk and out of the barracks.

"They're gonna shoot Ras. They're gonna shoot Ras." The chant went up from the two hundred and forty-one soldiers, who by then were standing in formation. The Germans dragged me through the mud and threw me into a solitary confinement cell. Six months earlier, anyone would have been shot who pulled a prank like that. But now the outcome of the war was in question and the Germans were being more careful with the American POWs.

I think that little stunt helped me keep my sanity. It also cured me from trying to win the war from my top bunk.

Sitting in my solitary cell, I thought about my family back home and wondered if I would ever get a letter from them. A thought about the postal service during wartime kept bouncing around in my mind: it seemed strange that letters go between the States and Germany when the two countries were at war. Millions of people were dying yet letters kept going back and forth between the two countries. For just six cents you could send a letter from Cedar, Michigan to Krems, Austria.

It seemed even more unusual that letters were delivered to a German prison camp. Certainly it took a long time for them to get there and a lot of them never made it. I wondered what the German postman thought when he picked up the letters at the post office that were destined for us. I wondered how many of my letters he "lost."

The Germans and the Americans censored every letter coming to, and leaving Stalag. Once, the guards burned boxes of letters in front of us because "they didn't have time to censor them." In the letters that we did receive, there could not be any news about Allied advances. If any of the parcels sent to us contained food, the guards kept it.

The ex-flyers wrote very little in their correspondence, or the German censors would not allow the letter to pass. The POWs were forbidden to write about the conditions in Stalag. Every letter the POWs wrote expressed how much they wanted to hear from their friends back home.

Meanwhile, three days later, I was escorted back to barracks 18. "You're not going to believe it, Ras," Charlie and Steiler greeted me. They were grinning ear to ear. "While you were resting in solitary confinement our troops landed at Normandy in France. They're calling in 'Operation Overlord.' Picked it up on a BBC broadcast."

"Mail call," the camp postman announced about then, and everyone filed into the barracks. Once the letters did arrive at Stalag they were separated by barracks and delivered by one of our POWs who was dubbed the "camp postman." All the POWs attended mail call in hope there was something for them.

"Steiler."

"Here."

"Comer."

"Right here." The names got called off until there was no more mail to deliver.

If your name was announced you were very happy, but when it wasn't you were very disappointed. You knew your family was writing even if your name wasn't called. During the sixteen months I was at Stalag, I received just two cards and one letter that didn't arrive until September 1944, ten months after I became a POW. I also got two packages: one from my family that contained four bars of soap, toothpaste and other usable items; and one from Bill and Mary Round, a box of cigars that proved valuable as a trading commodity. Each of us read our letters a hundred times and every letter was treated like a precious gem. Having a letter was the closest thing to being with your family.

Everyone would have kept the letters from family and friends, but it was rare that any of them made it back home. Paper was a valuable commodity in Stalag. We used it to write letters and make playing cards. Later we needed it to start fires on the forced march across Austria at the end of the war.

My dear friends the Scamehorns saved two of my letters and gave them to me as souvenirs after the war. I collected another one after the war and saved it for a keepsake; it was from my sister Phyllis and had been returned from Germany. The letter could not be delivered because there wasn't any prison left; before it could arrive the Russians had bombed the compound.

21

Show Time

IT WAS A MID-JULY DAY AND SOME OF THE POWS WERE strolling about between the barracks. Charlie came running like he had just seen Eisenhower. "Hey, Ras, the Swiss brought some musical instruments to camp. Word is that Commandant Kuhn said it's okay to let us have them. There's a horn among them." In no time, we filed into the main corridor that separated the two rows of barracks, just inside the main gate. In addition to the trumpet there was an accordion, three violins, and part of a drum set.

One of the German officers was explaining the terms that allowed us to keep the instruments.

"There must be no unruly behavior. There will be no playing the instruments after taps or before reveille. Lights must be out at the posted time. Any infringement of the rules and they will be confiscated."

"Hey Ras, you gonna show them how to play taps?" Charlie asked.

Several of the ex-flyers had been professional musicians before joining the army. By the end of the day two groups had formed. One trio called themselves the "Table Toppers." The name was derived from the tables that were used as a bandstand when they visited the different barracks. My group, the "Day Dreamers," jumped right into playing.

Hours later, with our backs to the gate and the boys gathered round, the "Day Dreamers" were playing patriotic songs like *Yankee Doodle Dandy* and *God Bless America*. A group of the guys started dancing when I launched into *Hot Lips*.

Everyone went silent when Kuhn and his fellow German officers walked up to the gate and glared at us. The festive mood died. We feared they might confiscate our new treasure. The silence hung heavy over the scene for a few minutes. Then, I loosened the valves on the trumpet, cleared the spit valve, blew a few practice notes, and started playing solo the notes to the *Battle Hymn of the Republic*. I slowed the tempo down quite a ways.

"Attention," Ken Kurtenbach ordered. The American flyers clicked their heels together and stood silently at attention, silently mouthing the words.

Mine eyes have seen the glory of the coming of the Lord:
He is trampling out the vintage where the grapes of wrath are stored:
He hath loosed the fateful lightning of His terrible swift sword:
His truth is marching on.
Glory, Glory, hallelujah!
Glory, Glory, hallelujah!
Glory, Glory, hallelujah!
His truth is marching on . . .

Everyone was staring at Kuhn. A moment of silence lasted an eternity. Then, the German hosts decided to leave us alone. The Commandant turned and walked away. Nobody said a word. After a short pause I commented, "First time I've ever played to a truly captive audience." That broke the ice and everyone laughed.

Among our talented POWs were writers, singers, dancers and artists. Best of all were the comedians. We used the talents of some playwrights to develop a show, and with some excellent voices and the band behind them, it was quite a performance. More than once, we spotted the German guards doing some toe tapping even to the *Star Spangled Banner*.

We also put up a theatre called the "Cardboard Playhouse." It was constructed of cardboard cartons that the Red Cross food parcels came in. By the time construction was done we had actors and actresses, that is to say, in some of the plays our soldiers dressed up as girls. They got lots of whistles and catcalls. Sometimes you did a double take to be sure you were still in an all-male prison. The kriegies who weren't in the plays became carpenters, electricians and stagehands who painted stages or scenery or helped get the stage ready for the next act. All the time the shows went on the German guards continually watched for us to break the rules so that they could repossess our instruments.

In November of 1944 we were allowed to put a loud speaker up in the camp. The system had come from Switzerland. Along with it the Swiss brought a record player and some recordings. It was a big issue between Ken Kurtenbach and Commandant Kuhn. After some tense negotiations Kuhn agreed to allow records to be played for a few hours each day. Some of the POWs managed to get a speaker hooked up in their own barracks and listen to American records while they rested in their bunks.

On Christmas 1944 and again on New Year's Eve the bands were allowed to play music all day long. It sounded as good as the music back home.

In January 1945 the Germans allowed a couple of old American films as well as a few French and German movies to be shown. The films actually had sex scenes that showed women's bodies. "Encore, encore!" The audience shouted as they applauded loudly.

Things had gotten a bit better in Stalag.

22

Word Home

OCTOBER 19, 1944 DAWNED AS A BRISK FALL MORNING. MOST of the POWs, including Charlie and I were hanging around outside the barracks.

"I wonder if college teams are playing football back home," Charlie said. He was sitting on one of the steps.

I was leaning against a post and reading my letter from home for the hundredth time. "Feels like football weather doesn't it?" I answered not looking up. "I'm not sure they're playing, but if they are I hope State beats Notre Dame."

"Wonder what's going on back in the States. You think our Mom and Dad know what it's like in here, Ras?"

That got my attention. Stalag was starting to get to Charlie too. "I'm sure they think about it a lot, Charlie."

The cool morning made me think of an October morning back in Michigan. For a moment I thought I was home. During fall in northern Michigan the oak and maple trees are beautiful, dressed in yellow and crimson colors. I looked around. There wasn't anything inside the wired perimeter of Stalag that had any color to change. But, outside the leaves on the trees near the cemetery were turning color.

Unbeknownst to me, my status as a prisoner had just been reported in the local paper back home. My parents had just received word by Harold Sheehan about conditions in Stalag. After Normandy and the advance of the Allies, the German High Command was beginning to bargain more aggressively with the West using the American POWs as one of their chits. Hal was one of those chits sent home.

I took time away from reading to recall Hal's words. "I'm getting out of here!" Hal announced as he hobbled out of barracks 32 back on a hot and dusty July day. "The Germans have arranged to exchange a group of wounded American POWs with some of theirs back in the States." Everyone crowded around to hear the details. The Red Cross arranged for the prisoner exchange between Americans and the Germans. Hal got out of Stalag on July 25, along with ten other badly wounded POWs, and was repatriated. Along with ten other ex-flyers, he was transported to Sweden where the exchange took place and then sent on to the States aboard a ship named the Gripsholm.

"What should I tell your folks, Ras?" Hal asked. The Germans had already briefed them on not saying anything bad about Stalag or no more exchanges would occur. "I don't mind calling your family and telling them how things are in here."

"Tell them that I'm doing fine. There's no point in having them worry about me. Besides, it's probably the best thing for the soldiers here. The Germans are starting to loosen up a bit."

It wasn't until three months later, in mid-October, that Hal got stateside. He called my parents and told them I was in good health. He also told them the food wasn't too bad and that I hadn't lost any weight. "No, none of your parcels got through," Hal told my Dad. "Nor has anyone else's." It was one of the more disappointing bits of news Hal carried home. Besides Hal, four of the other released flyers who got stateside wrote my parents.

I went back to reading my letter. I had turned twenty-four in August and treated my one and only letter as a belated birthday present.

I thought about what Charlie had said on my birthday. "How many more birthdays you think we're gonna celebrate in here?" Birthdays weren't celebrated in Stalag. The soldiers didn't light candles or sing songs like they did at Christmas. "Let's eat a D-bar and pretend to have a party."

"Good idea," I told him "We can pretend it's a chocolate birthday cake." But that was the extent of our partying.

23

Kick-A-Poo Juice

LEANING AGAINST THE POST, I WAS THINKING ABOUT HOW lucky Hal was to be back in the States and what we could do to have a little fun in Stalag.

"Hey Charlie, I've got an idea on how to celebrate the coming new year," I said.

"That so, Ras, what ya' got in mind?" Charlie asked.

"Let's make some kick-a-poo juice and get smashed."

"Sounds good," Charlie said. He didn't give the idea much credence until ten other POWs decided to throw in on the mixture.

"Getting caught means a stay in solitary," Charlie said, now smiling.

"We need a place to hide it and some way to store it," Cecil Comer had joined in.

"What are we gonna make it in, Ras?" Charlie asked.

Graham came up with the first answer. "Several unpunctured cans from the Red Cross packages."

"Why not take the chow tub and have the boys in the kitchen get another one?" Charlie asked.

"Too risky," I answered. "The Germans will know if one of the tubs is missing." For any project of this magnitude there was bound to be a lot of deliberations. Because we had a lot of free time and little to do, any idea was likely to generate a lot of discussion.

"All right, I got it," said Graham. "How about getting a piece of plywood and cut it into five pieces to make a pail, say six inches in diameter and," he hesitated, scratched his chin, then added, "maybe twenty inches tall. We cut a piece for the bottom and glue it to the sides."

"That's great Graham," Charlie said. "Why don't you just go over to Commandant Kuhn and ask him for some wood and a saw. And while you're at it get some airplane glue. Better yet, why don't you ask him for some vintage French champagne so we won't have to make our own brew? I'm sure he's got plenty of it."

"Wait a minute," I said. "Graham's onto something. We've got the wood."

"Where?" Comer asked.

"From our bunks. One of us loses a bunk board. If the juice turns out good it'll be worth it."

"How is this so-called pail going to be held together?" Comer asked.

"If we carve it carefully and fit rags into the seams and apply some oleo margarine for caulk, it won't leak. There's enough electrical wire around to bind it together," I said.

Everyone was getting a little excited that this was one idea that might actually work.

"Okay," Charlie said, cogitating a bit. "We'll have a lottery to see who gives up their board. I'll write one through ten on ten pieces of paper. On the back of one of them will be an X. You guys each pick a number. I get the number not picked. That sound fair enough?"

Graham picked first. "Seven," he said.

Charlie started to laugh. "I knew whoever picked first would lose. Seven was bound to be the first number picked and it's got the X on it. Serves you right Graham. After all it was your idea to build a wooden pail."

It took a week just to carve the board into the pieces needed to make the pail. All the time the carving was going on rags were being greased with margarine. Charlie ripped some unused electrical wire out of the barracks. When it was tested, the pail was a real piece of work.

"I got the perfect hiding place for this liquid gold," Charlie said. "Take off a floorboard near the corner of the barracks. Put the board back after sliding the pail of juice underneath. The guards will never find it during inspection."

Everything was ready to go into production. Each of the ten partners contributed something fermentable. The occasional Red Cross parcel we received contained a box of raisins or prunes along with orange paste and sugar. A prune was worth fourteen raisins or a teaspoon of orange paste or six cubes of sugar. We also bargained with the Italians trading cigarettes for two raw potatoes. Each time contents were added, the pail was filled back up with water. The older the contents got, the more they fermented. The more they fermented, the more the aroma permeated the air. No one got a taste. The penalty of tasting was it would be your only taste.

"It's the middle of November," Graham said after the kick-a-poo juice had started to ferment, "if we're still POWs on December 31st, then the bubbly's gonna help usher in the New Year!"

But first there was a little matter of the camp boxing championship to settle.

24

Happy New Year

"I CAN BEAT ANYONE IN STALAG," BOASTED OF JUSTIN Shalinski of barracks 35. Justin wasn't particularly tall, only five feet eight inches, weight 165 pounds. He was a city boy who had played linebacker and boxed for a small college in Kentucky. Justin also carried a long jagged scar over the bridge of his nose, courtesy of a crash landing and no suturing by the German doctors. Every barracks followed with a nomination to the "strongest man in Stalag" boast and the boxing championship was underway. The scar across the bridge of Shalinski's nose made him look all the tougher. Graham was our nominee. The kriegies quickly made a boxing ring.

The rules were simple and were explained by the referee. "Three rounds with a one-minute rest between rounds, no hitting below the belt, no holding, a knockdown wins. If both soldiers make it to the end of the third round standing, then the fight's a draw."

The "bell" rang when the designated POW yelled, "Bell." Bookies were out in force.

"This is great," I said to Charlie. "Shalinski's got a big mouth. Our farm boy is not about to get beat. There's real bounty to be made here with some well timed wagering."

It was on December 15, 1944 when Shalinski jumped into the ring elbows up, fists up, bobbing and weaving and looking very much the prizefighter. Graham was much slower, watching Shalinski carefully, arms circling from the sides. Three rounds later, both warriors were standing, the fight in a draw and Shalinski with a bloody nose. No one in camp had seen as many smiles in a long time. Graham and Shalinski jovially walked out of the ring with their arms around each other. No one had lost a bet and everyone was patting each other on the back. The kriegies from both barracks claimed that they would have won if the fight had gone a full ten rounds.

With the permission of Commandant Kuhn, the "Day Dreamers" played Christmas songs that were broadcast over the camp's loudspeaker on December 25th. Kuhn also had agreed that the "Day Dreamers" could help welcome in the New Year by playing again on December 31st. The kriegies were in a little more festive mood than they had been a year earlier. We had managed to get reports of the advancing allied troops both from the Red Cross representatives and an occasional BBC broadcast.

This New Year's Eve wasn't going to be the same as the last one. Ten of us intended to usher it in with a little kick-a-poo juice just before lights went out along with a song of *Auld Lang Syne*. It was right after a dinner of black bread and barley soup that we dug out our liquid treasure. What we had concocted or what it might do when consumed was unknown to anyone, but we had waited anxiously the last two months for tonight to arrive.

"All right," Charlie said. "An equal amount in each can and chug-a-lug."

I'm not sure what proof the juice ended up being, but everyone who toasted the New Year that fateful night quickly lost all good reasoning, speech and mobility.

"To the advancing Allied armies," Charlie's toasted.

Cecil chimed in. "May the B-17s continue to bomb Germany." With each toast we took another chug.

Graham let out a belch before he offered up his. "Happy New Year to our families back home."

"Here, here," Charlie replied.

I raised my can. "May all measure of bad things befall Commandant Kuhn."

We fell into our bunks, room spinning. Less than two hours later Charlie and I started vomiting. I thought we were done for.

"I think I'm gonna puke my guts out," Charlie said.

Graham's was holding his head. "My head's splitting."

All ten of us ended up at Camp Lazaret (Stalag's field hospital) and had our stomachs pumped out. Graham drank the most and almost died. When they stuck tubes down into our stomachs and pumped them out it was bad enough, but the hangover was even worse. The guards saw fit to try to make us remember never to break the rules again by sentencing each of us to a five-day stay in solitary confinement.

25

Spring Break

IT WAS STILL DARK AND THUNDERING, BUT HADN'T STARTED to rain. It was an early March, 1945 morning. Jimmy Blake, an ex-flyer from Ohio, was standing at the end of the roll call line just behind one of the German guards. He had some dirt in his fist making a funnel to send it down the barrel of the guard's rifle. I couldn't help smiling as I nudged the POW next to me, and with a nod of my head, pointed out what was happening. Before long everyone from barracks 18 who had filed out for roll call was getting a silent chuckle. Just then, wham, a rifle butt to the back of Jimmy's head from another guard sent him sprawling, blood running down from the back of his head. Jimmy was dragged away unconscious for a three-day stint in solitary. While they were dragging him away it started to rain.

Once we were back inside our barracks Comer started the conversation. "I wish we could pay them back for what they did to Jimmy," he said.

"I know just what the doctor called for." I was staring down at the table and sipping dark tea. It was an idea that I had been kicking around in my head ever since Kurtenbach asked me to be chairman of the escape committee. I was surprised that they hadn't found someone new for the job since no one had gotten out of Stalag during my tenure. Now I had a chance to earn my stripes. "If it keeps raining, then we're getting out of here tonight, all of us."

"What?" Charlie said. "You know something we don't? How we gonna make the break?" The other kriegies quickly gathered around.

"Yep, there's gonna be a big break tonight," I said. "Pass the word." I paused to let the idea settle in. "The Krauts will be out there in full force, patrolling the whole night." There must have been fifty POWs around the table when I looked up. "We're going to have a little fun tonight."

I hustled through the rain over to barracks 37 and ran the idea past Kurtenbach. It was one of the few times in Stalag that everyone agreed on an idea. Word quickly spread about the planned break. We acted excited and talked enough about escaping that the guards got wind of it. That night, lights went out at nine o'clock. By then it was raining hard. A cold wind had picked up and sent ripples across the top of the mud puddles.

Guard duty had increased. There were extra guards in the towers with their lights circling the compound. Extra guards in their long trench coats, along with their German shepherds and Doberman pinschers, patrolled the perimeter. It was quite a show. All the ex-flyers were tucked away in their barracks and got to watch it. For once, we had gotten the better of our captors, who were cold, wet, and tired.

"When do you think we will get out of here for real, Ras?" Charlie asked.

"Any day now, Charlie. I reckon we'll see Ike pull up to the front gate in a tank with a convoy of trucks to take us away." But I really didn't have any idea.

26

Forced March

I SAW MORE GERMAN GENERALS DURING THE FIRST DAYS IN April 1945 than American generals during the entire war. German officers were arriving at Stalag 17B daily. "The Russian army is shooting American POWs," one of them announced. "You will prepare to evacuate the camp. When the order is given, you will march orderly and with due haste to the Fatherland." By this time there wasn't much the Germans said that we believed. For all the captured American flyers knew, this "pep talk" about the Russians was a lie, and was just a way to get us to cooperate with the Germans when the time came. Still, evacuating Stalag was music to our ears.

"Come over here!" Steiler shouted as I walked into the barracks. Everyone was glued to the crystal set.

"The Russians are making a pincer movement around Vienna in eastern Austria on their march toward Berlin." It was a BBC announcer. The Russian Army was within ten miles of Stalag, driving on the town of St. Polten, a moderate size Austrian city about fifteen miles south of Krems. We were certain that the Russians were getting close because the flare of big guns could be seen on the horizon at night. For several days we had watched and listened to the heavy artillery fire both to the east and to the south. B-24s bombed Krems that same week. We could see the bombs as they fell.

Under peacetime conditions, the foothills of the Alps are picturesque. You can hike from the birthplace of Mozart at Salzburg to the birthplace of Hitler at Braunau. The countryside has vines growing everywhere, producing grapes that turn into fine Austrian merlot or chardonnay wines that could be enjoyed at another time. Medieval castles speckle the landside. The Danube River runs through the countryside. In the late 1800s Johann Strauss wrote the *Blue Danube*, a waltz. Durnstein, a beautiful medieval town just west of Krems, sits on the Danube. It holds the ruins of the fort where King Richard the Lionhearted was imprisoned in 1192, on his way home from a crusade. Unfortunately for us, it was war. The "orderly" hike that the POWs were commanded to take "with due haste" was a forced march.

Like the other American soldiers, Charlie and I let out a hoot when we heard the announcement. Everyone was excited. "I can't believe my ears. We're finally getting outta here!" Charlie said.

"Me either," I said. "But you know something, Charlie," I was watching the celebration. "It isn't gonna be that easy."

"How so?"

"It's a long way to Germany and you notice the general said 'march.' He didn't say we were going to be transported." Some of the POWs were dancing. Charlie and I watched them having fun and thought about what was ahead of us.

On April 4, 1945 the German officer's order was confirmed. Stalag became a madhouse. Trading between the prisoners and over the fence with the Italians was at a frenzy. Bonfires raged all day and into the night. Anything we couldn't carry with us was burned.

If the ex-flyers knew what was in store for them, they would have opted for a night's sleep instead. In Stalag there was no country store to visit and stock up on provisions. The most important staple was water but we had no way to carry it. A few of the kriegies had buckets. Others made water bags from burlap sacks that were lined with margarine, attached with a rope, and tied to a pole; so two men could carry it on their shoulders as they walked. The margarine slowed down the leaking but it still didn't hold water very long. Its only real value was to fill it in a stream and drink it relatively quickly on the march. The rest of us drank when possible and from what we could.

"We need to hide new tin cans from the Red Cross parcels and keep the guards from punching holes in them," I told Charlie. "At least we'll have something to carry water in."

"And all the food from the parcels," Charlie added. "It's the only food we'll be able to carry."

"Yep," I said. "Good idea. I've got three bars of soap, a hundred thirty-two cigarettes, and four cigars. Maybe I'll be we can bargain with the guards, or even some of the locals along the way for something to eat."

The German guards weren't much better off than the POWs. With the German economy almost totally destroyed, there wasn't enough food for everyone. There weren't enough provisions for the officers and fighting troops for the High Command to worry about the prison guards escorting us. They were too low in the German military pecking order to get any food. The guards were forced to confiscate food from civilians and from us.

"You're not taking my food," yelled one of our soldiers. A Czech guard named Policheck hit him in the face with the butt of his rifle, knocking out some teeth, just for a little orange pulp and a few raisins. Some of the guards were like that and hurt unarmed prisoners. Policheck made it on the short list with a number of our soldiers. It was going to be a long march. A number of the POWs weren't going to survive. Four of the German guards died on the march as well.

"Have you got any idea how to get my film out without the Germans finding it?" Ben Phelper asked. By now Ben had taken a lot of very valuable pictures.

"Sure, I'll carve out the heel of my clog and seal it inside," I told him. The Germans never found it. (After the war, Ben published the photos in *Kriegie Memories.)*

April 5, 1945. "You will leave the compound," Commandant Kuhn announced over the loudspeaker at morning roll call, before dawn. The British, French, Poles, Russian, Italian and Serbs, along with over two hundred German quards, got similar orders.

"Take whatever you can carry," German guards ordered as they scurried through the barracks. Some of the prisoners were a little nervous, not certain what the real intentions of the Germans were.

At precisely seven o'clock Commandant Kuhn ordered, "fall out."

In rows of three we left Stalag 17B, eight groups with over five hundred American POWs in each group, most men laden with an unpunctured empty can, a few unopened cans of powdered mild and liver paste or whatever else the kriegie stored to eat, and a blanket. The column marched west, away from the cemetery where Paige Gillerman and the POWs from other nationalities lay. It took physical and inward strength to endure. We quickly found out what poor conditions we were in. The ex-flyers had already lost weight and were deconditioned from their stay in Stalag. Starting from the northeast Austrian border, we marched through the foothills of the Alps towards southeast Germany.

"You will walk for fifty minutes and then rest for ten," the guard informed us. We marched for twenty-two miserable days. Footwear, or the lack of it, became problematic early in the march. None of us had combat fatigues and no one had combat issue shoes. Like many other kriegies, I had wooden clogs. Cecil's clogs were at least two sizes too big for his feet. "My feet are starting to blister," he said on the first day. Unable to heal, sores got worse by the day.

Each day the direction of our march changed. We were headed west, but if either the American troops or Russian Army were having success we had to march north or south for a few hours. Knowing our troops were advancing kept our spirits high. The Germans didn't give us anything to eat for three days. Then they issued each kriegie two potatoes and a few specks of salt. No one complained. The spuds weren't cooked but we still savored every bite.

To most people, diarrhea is just a twenty-four hour stomach bug that can be dealt with at home by drinking ginger ale or tea. When our clothes got soiled we lived in them. Sometimes at night, when one of the boys or their sack-mates couldn't control themselves, they woke with their blankets smelling like the latrine. "When I got the runs at home, they'd only last a day or two," Graham said. "Now, it's six to ten times a day. I don't care anymore if anyone sees me go. There ain't no privacy." Graham's deep voice carried over the entire column. Our soldiers didn't care much about privacy; they were already accustomed to the 24-holer at Stalag. "What I am worried about is my butt, because it burns," Graham's voice resonated. "It burns more every time I have to go." It would have been nice, but it was not possible, to be clean. There was no paper to wipe with. "Use leaves instead of paper," Graham said. "It's either that, or use your left hand to wipe with and clean your hand in the dirt."

On the forced march, the soldiers who had dysentery had to run to the front of the column as often and as fast as their stomach cramps told them to do so. "I'm taking a speedy walk to the front of the column, step out, and take a quick crap," Graham said. The POW couldn't step out of formation and have the column pass him by. A German would ram him with the butt of his rifle or even a bayonet. Multiply that fiasco a few score and it was the true race of all races.

Falling out at the end of the day meant three of us teaming up together. "You, me and Charlie," Comer suggested. "We can put one blanket on the ground and use two for covers." I always liked our waist gunner but he got the better of me on that deal. Each night, I had to fight for my fair share of the covers or they ended up around Comer.

We had just filed out on the fourth day of the march. "Look at that!" Charlie was pointing to an American P-51 flying overhead. To an American fighter plane a column of soldiers is an inviting target. The soldiers in one of our groups spread out an American flag. "He's tipping his wings," Cecil said. "That means he's knows who we are." Some of the POWs managed to cheer. After passing through Poggstall the column halted on a deserted farm. Some of us slept in an old barn. The wooden floor was a welcome relief from the cold, damp ground. Thinking about the P-51 made the ex-flyers fell better that night than at any other time in the march.

"Now that one of our fighters has spotted us, it should only be a day or two before we'll be free." It was the wishful thought of one of our soldiers.

"Bivouac and remain here for the day," the guards ordered the next morning. "You will be allowed a day of rest."

"We're just sitting here staring at each other," Graham said after hours had passed. "They want us to think we're getting a rest, but I'll bet it's to keep us off the road so we don't get in the way of German regulars."

Four thousand two hundred American soldiers had started the march in eight groups all within a half a mile of each other. By the sixth day, there was up to a half a mile between each of the eight groups. From start to finish the column was over four miles long. As it so happened, it was not a good day to be strung out. Passing through Isperdorf we encountered SS troops standing next to their tanks, studying maps. The SS glared at us with icy stares that had vengeance written all over them. There was no holding back as we literally ran pass them and through the town. "I wouldn't want to run into those troops even if I was armed," I said to Charlie. "Even the German guards seem to be afraid of them." After reaching the outskirts of the town, the guards conferred. They looked confused. "Look at them, Charlie. They haven't got a clue where to camp and no way to keep us fed or sheltered. They've got no water and no firewood. The little food they do have, they keep mostly for themselves."

April 12, 1945, seven days into the march, a cold rain that had started during the night became mixed with snow and the boys shivered as they marched along the north side of the Danube. Near the end of the day the column was ordered off the road into a three-story crop-drying building. The structure was well constructed with a solid roof and cement floors. The sidewalls were separated to let the wind and sun enter. "At least we'll be out of the wet snow," Charlie said. Charlie, Comer and I were at the end of the first floor.

Just outside from where the three of us bedded down was a small hut. As darkness approached Charlie said, "Look Ras, a German soldier is going into that small shed. It looks like he's dropping off some kind of package."

"I'll bet anything it's a bomb," Comer said moments later. "What a perfect way to kill us all. They can blame it on a RAF night raid."

"We got to get it out of there!" Charlie was already on his feet. The three of us slithered through an opening in the sidewall and ran to the shed.

"Look, it's a bag of powdered pea soup complete with a bucket!" I exclaimed.

"Gee, we can't judge all the German soldiers to be the same," Charlie said. "If that guy gets caught, he'll certainly be shot for giving food away."

"If I were looking at you two back in the States, I'd give you something to eat!" Comer joked. I looked at Cecil. The waist gunner's nervous laugh was hiding his weakening condition. We scraped up the cleanest snow possible and melted it in the bucket, mixed in the ingredients and spread our good fortune around with the other POWs as far as it would stretch.

"I want to thank our benefactor," Graham said lapping down the cold pea soup. He repeated himself several times.

It was lucky that we received the extra food, for the ninth day turned warm and the column marched over twenty miles, the farthest of any day. If our rest stops were at a stream, then the boys soaked their feet. "My feet are getting bad," Cecil said. "At least the cold water will numb my sores for a while." Cecil's feet had swollen to the point that his clogs had become tight. Many of our soldiers were suffering the same malady.

"Rouse," the usual German command. Ten minutes had passed and the guards were very punctual. Within the hour we came across bits of American warplanes strewn all along the side of the road. "What do you think happened to their crews?" I asked Charlie. We were looking at a star from a B-17 lying on the ground on what was the only remaining piece of a fuselage, a B-17 star that made a lasting impression on the ex-flyers as they marched past. Bomb craters surrounded what looked like the remains of an armament plant. A residential area we passed after the plant had also been bombed. Just like London, only chimneys stood, the sole survivors of the incendiary bombing. "They shouldn't have put houses so near that plant," Charlie said.

The little city of Mauthausen lies just east of Linz. This late in the war, the Nazis encouraged the civilian population to hang the captured American and British flyers who had parachuted from their damaged craft. The local police lacked control. After the war, the Allies held the civil authorities responsible for the flyers' deaths. The German guards wound us around the city to avoid angry crowds.

"Jesus, look at that!" Charlie said. The column had halted despite the commands from the German guards to keep marching. We were staring at the pinnacle of the Third Reich. Immediately in front of us was the Mauthausen Concentration Camp. Dead bodies in striped uniforms littered the ground outside the walls of the camp. Other prisoners were laboring in the yard and being whipped if they fell down or couldn't work any longer. Comer, Graham, and the other soldiers who had stopped in front of the camp, were staring at the partially clad corpses, corpses with heads that looked too big for their trunks, heads with shrunken temples. Their knees looked too big for their legs and their feet were bare, not even wooden clogs. They were broken bodies. Their grim faces revealed that their spirits had been broken too.

"What's this all about, Ras?" Charlie asked.

"I don't know Charlie, but whatever it is, it isn't good," I replied just as one of the guards thrust a rifle butt between my shoulder blades, knocking me to the ground. I turned quickly, angry, and looked him square in the eyes. It was the German guard who had the frightened look on his face, not me. There would be no hiding these atrocities from the world and the Germans knew it. The American Army was closing too quickly on Mauthausen and the city did not appear to be militarily fortified. There wasn't going to be enough time to dispose of the concentration camp and those left in it. That night the men were very quiet in camp. Many of them were afraid and didn't sleep after what they had seen.

Twenty-three days after we passed the Mauthausen concentration camp, the American infantry liberated those who survived. Our soldiers gave them clean water to drink and sugar cubes to suck on.

We were up at dawn, once again, to march across northern Austria toward the Fatherland. The next morning's march started in silence, images from yesterday still vivid, until a buxom Austrian woman on a bike passed the column. "Milk wagon coming through," was the shout from ahead of us. "Milk wagon passing," as she pedalled passed, all the guys staring at her. "Milk wagon coming," you could hear from behind. All the boys laughed. It helped a lot to be light hearted at times, just like we had been in Stalag 17B.

Flyers know the different sounds made by approaching aircraft. "It's Russian fighters," yelled one of the POWs. "Run for those trees!" Russian fighters were approaching in a strafing formation from the east, approaching what they believed to be a column of German infantry. We were defenseless except for the light machine-gun fire of the German guards.

"They're leaving, Ras," Charlie shouted after the fighters had made one pass.

"They're low on fuel, Charlie, or we'd have 'em on our backs all morning," I said. Near the end of the day we crossed the Danube heading north to south. When night came, the POWs got their first real sleep in the last three nights.

"You will bivouac next to the road," one of the German guards ordered the column. We had passed through Steyregg before reaching Linz. There the guards got pigs that they butchered and cooked that night. But the POWs got only the scent from their cooking as we lay at the edge of a field.

"Do you believe what we're looking at, Charlie?" I asked. Twenty feet from us across the shell-marked road was a large area, recently planted with potatoes. Our stomachs growled. The potato plants were spread out in a jagged pattern. There weren't any leaves on the plants, just little shoots sticking out of the aged potatoes that had been planted in the ground. Looking closely, we could see the top of the potato sticking out of the ground from where the shoot had grown.

When sleep came, the only light was came from the small fires the guards had started.

"Let's go," I said. Charlie, Comer and I crawled across the road and dug up as many of the potatoes as possible in the few minutes we had. We were careful not to wake anyone or cause a commotion that would get the attention of the guards. The potatoes were all old and brown. Some were very soft. But we gobbled them down quickly.

The following morning Dyer whispered, "I never knew old potatoes tasted so good," as we rolled up our blankets. We stopped talking and stared at a fellow POW who was eating some of our discarded potato peels. When you're starving, almost anything that is growing, or has grown, becomes a tempting meal. I even tried grass clippings but couldn't keep them down.

"Halt," the German guard ordered. It was early the afternoon of the thirteenth day.

"You will move into that open field." The column had just reached Linz and was ordered into the field while the Germans decided on a route through the city. Unfortunately for us, that was an afternoon our B-17s decided to attack Linz. There were hours of constant pounding. We found some protection by piling four and five deep next to a rock fence that stretched for several hundred feet on the edge of the field. When night came the RAF continued the attack.

The darkness also brought German trucks pulling artillery. Lights out, they bumped along the crater-marked road next to the field. "How can they see where they're going?" I asked Graham.

"I've been waiting for this," Graham said.

"Waiting for what?" I asked. Graham nodded at the approaching Sergeant Stein.

It was Stein who had tried to provoke a confrontation with Graham in Stalag. There was a lot of confusion with the RAF bombing run and the movement of the German trucks. As Stein passed, Graham knocked him in front of one of the large trucks. It killed him instantly. Even I was startled at how fast Graham moved. Stein hadn't seen him coming.

"You got lucky, Graham," I said. The German regulars must not have seen what happened or were in too big of a hurry to care. Whatever the reason, the truck column didn't even stop. Another dead body didn't attract much attention.

"I told you I wasn't going to forget that guy."

At dawn we marched through Linz, surveying the destruction from the previous day's raid. Fires started by the incendiary bombs were still burning. Air raid sirens sounded and our cadence hastened. Angry civilians confronted us once again with accusations of "fliegerganster." German regulars also confronted us with, "Why did you bomb women and children?" It was always better if the Americans said nothing and moved quickly along. We continued southwest on a collision course with American General Gerow's 13th Armored Division, which was heading east towards Linz. We got through Linz and back into open countryside.

On April 19, 1945, fourteen days into the march, we passed an airfield manned by Hungarians. There were German Me-109s and Me-210s fighters on the ground. American P-38s flew over but none of the German fighter planes went up to engage them. The Hungarians were waiting for the more valuable P-51s to risk damage to their own craft.

"If they're smart," I told Charlie, "they need to ask themselves if they want to risk dying when they can't possibly win the war." Our P-51 was the dominant fighter in the sky. "No matter what the Hungarians have been ordered to do, the only thing they should do is run and hide."

"Charlie," I said. "Look at the change in the German guards. They look more determined, almost as if they have a sense of impending doom. You can see it in their faces and hear it in their voices. They want to move west as quickly as possible and put some distance between them and the advancing Russian army. The Russians want a pound of flesh and those guys know it." It was clear that the guards were under orders to get as many of us as possible to Braunau, as quickly as possible. Only Eisenhower had a magic wand that could save the German troops from the Russians. We were pawns on the German chessboard and soon it was going to be checkmate. Some of our soldiers couldn't keep up and were allowed to ride in horse-drawn wagons.

"Unless they're going to transport our disabled soldiers by truck," I told Charlie, "there's simply no way we can move any faster."

The following morning was bright and sunny, unlike any previous day. "Did you sleep okay, Charlie?" I asked. Charlie had a blank look on his face as he searched for an answer. I actually managed to laugh out loud, as I waited for his response. None of us ever slept okay. German troops crossing a mile in front of us kept the formation from starting our daily hike. To keep the ex-flyers from trying to leave the formation, the Germans passed the word that armed guards were following us, and that others were two to three hundred feet on each side of the road. "You will be shot without warning if you attempt to escape." We lived under the same rules at Stalag.

"Charlie, Charlie" I whispered. "I'm going to find some groceries."

"You're nuts," he said. "There's roving guards. You'll be shot on sight."

Right or wrong, I was hungry enough to take the chance. With the guards watching the troop movements, I was on my way. After enduring Stalag with a measured amount of caution, in retrospect, this decision was possibly my worst. Besides the roving German guards, if the advancing Allies or Russian troops saw me, they would think I was a German soldier and probably shoot. Still, I was hungry enough to take the chance.

Not having any idea where to go, I just moved out at a ninety-degree angle from the formation and walked across the fields and woods for two miles where I came upon some farm buildings. I thought at the time that someone was watching over me and if a shot had rung out, it would not reach me, let alone hit me. Three people were standing near a mound of dirt that had smoke coming out of the top. As I moved closer, they made a run for the protection of some nearby buildings. The mound of dirt turned out to be an outside clay oven. After standing there for several minutes, a door to one of the buildings nearest me opened. A buxom, middle-aged woman came out to see who this stranger was. Her eyes told her thoughts: relief that I wouldn't or couldn't hurt them, disgust for the way I looked, and pity for a starving man. With my best German lingo, I tried hard to convince her to give me some food.

"Ich bin hungry," I said pointing at the oven and motioning to my mouth. My knowledge of the language didn't allow me to tell her where I had come from but bless her; she understood why I was there. Within minutes, I was off with my newfound riches of bread and eggs.

Graham, Charlie and Comer were waiting, hoping for my return. I had been gone almost four hours. It was Graham who greeted me. "You got my vote, Ras. I thought you'd either bought the farm or you were headed for home. Charlie and Cecil said you'd lost your marbles to do something like that. Huh, huh, huh, huh." He was nodding his approval. Dyer had disapproved at what I had done and just stared at me.

"Look what I've got for you," I said, producing an egg each for each of them and the loaf of bread that was quickly devoured.

Charlie drank his egg. The expression on his face had changed. "I told these guys, right after you left," he contradicted Graham, "that you'd probably get lucky."

One of our soldiers had picked up the BBC on his crystal set. "Advancing American and Russian troops just met seventy miles south of Berlin," the broadcaster said. Word passed through the column. The coffin lid was being hammered shut on Nazi Germany. The reign of the Third Reich was about to end. For those of us who survived the forced march, trip home was in the making. That night the POWs housed in an old aluminum factory, a vacant shell of a building that had escaped the bombings. The factory was silent. There was no manufacturing capability left in Austria; American and British bombers had seen to that.

On April 26, 1945, twenty-one days into the march, rain fell as reached the borders of Austria and Germany. There we were corralled in the Leach Forest due to the advance of our 13th Armored Division, who chose to shell the area. The forest was being overrun with three divisions of German infantry retreating west. "I'm using my tin can to dig a hole," I told Charlie. It was during the first volley of the American artillery. Most of our soldiers were doing the same thing.

On its twenty-second day, the march ended in the Leach Forest at the juncture of the Inn and Salzach rivers, two hundred eighty-one miles from Stalag. By that time, all the POWs understood priorities: shelter, obtaining food, waste management, and getting wood to burn. "Barracks thirty-three to thirty-six build shelters," Kurtenbach barked out. We were issued a limited number of axes for our soldiers to cut down trees. Despite the rain, those soldiers who were strong enough got right to work. The shelters included crude log cabins, a house for Red Cross parcels that were sure to come, and even a field hospital.

"Those from barracks 15 and 16 build latrines." Large rectangular holes were dug in the ground. Around the opening logs were connected in the same rectangular shape about twelve inches above the ground. When a soldier had to go, he squatted on a log along with many of the other POWs.

Water and food were another thing. There was plenty to drink but no realistic means to store it. There were no rations, of course.

The French, Russian, English, Serbs, and Poles all began making shelters as well. "You will place logs be on the ground to serve as borders," the German guards ordered. It was their attempt to keep order and try and to segregate the different nationalities.

Several of us worked our way down to the Inn River that forms the border between Austria and Germany. From our vantage point, on a bluff overlooking the river, we could see American tanks traveling east. A small village, in the route that the tanks were heading, was flying white flags.

"It's time to go," I said. "Those are our tanks down there."

"And what about our escort service?" Charlie asked. "They might be a little upset if they can't deliver us as planned. If we run, they might decide to do away with as many of us as they can."

"I can't run," Cecil said.

"All right," I said a moment later. "Charlie and I will try to get to our troops. Cecil, we'll send one of those tanks back here to give you a ride home." Other flyers joined us.

27

The Way Home

"POP, POP, POP." THE RAPID MACHINE GUN FIRE BROKE THE water in front of us. Thirty-three POWs had made a run for it. We ducked for cover in a marsh, knee deep in the cold Inn River. Anytime was a bad time to get killed, but this time would be particularly bad with the end of the war in sight. A pontoon bridge that our forces had constructed was nearby. After resting for several hours and watching the landscape, Charlie and I crawled out of the brush at the river's edge, crossed the bridge and headed south along the road, hoping to meet up with our infantry. The rest of the POWs followed a short time later.

"Look!" Charlie shouted. "German soldiers heading our way!" We had taken a turn in the road and were walking straight toward three German regulars. Lucky for us, they were anxious to give up their guns and grenades. It was a real turn about. "I'm not sure if they've pulled the pins on the grenades," Charlie said. He pointed one of their side arms at them and motioned for them to dispose of the grenades in the river. Then we continued south while the Germans headed north.

A few minutes later an American tank rumbled down the road straight at us and stopped. A corporal appeared in the open conning tower. It was an unusual situation, looking down the gun barrel of an

American tank with an American GI pointing his rifle at us. The excitement of running into one of our own tanks and being with our own soldiers was overwhelming. I wanted to kiss the big tank. The corporal had a perplexed look on his face seeing three unkempt GIs in Serb uniforms and German side arms, all with big smiles on their faces.

"William E. Rasmussen, Staff Sergeant, United States Air Force," I said saluting. Charlie did the same. "Are we glad to see you. Which way is the shortest route back to our troops?"

"Continue southwest. Use this road. Proceed with caution. In very short order you'll run into our main tank column. Our troops are right behind them," the corporal answered matter-of-factly.

"Could you spare some rations?" Charlie asked.

He looked at us, saying something inaudible to the men in the tank. "The only things we have are ten and one rations, sir." His expression hadn't changed and he was still pointing his rifle at us.

"That will do just fine, Corporal," I told him. He took his bayonet, reached over the tower and cut a box loose. "Charlie, this'll be the best food we've had in over a year and a half," I said. It included canned ham and vegetables.

Charlie quickly told the tank crew a short story about how we had spent the last month.

"There's a lot of our guys up in that forest," he said pointing back at the Leach Forest. "In fact, there are over 4,000 of them." The corporal related that bit of information to the tank crew who got on the radio to command.

"General Gerow has been notified," the corporal said, now saluting. Our POWs were on their way home.

Charlie and I continued walking and were joined by other POWs who by this time were coming out of the forest in droves. The guards were leaving as fast as they could. Even though we enjoyed the few hours of extra freedom, had we waited, we would have saved the energy used with our early escape. As we walked along the road a Jeep came toward us with a public address system booming. It was General Gerow, Commander 13th Armored Unit, who issued orders.

"You are to head south to the village of Ranshofen where you will be fed, clothed and moved on to a hospital within twenty-four hours for a medical checkup. In the best interests of our soldiers and the civilian population, you are all ordered to avoid contact with them and any of their belongings. There is to be no action taken against the civilian population. Do not incite them to riot." Then he roared away.

"Listen to him," Charlie said. "Generals haven't changed. Instead of welcoming us back they're worried about looting. All I want to do is take a shower, get deloused and get into a clean uniform."

"Everything is a matter of priorities to the generals, Charlie," I said. "I hope they find time to arrest the guards who escorted us here." It was a wish that never came true.

The American Colonel who liberated our soldiers in the forest couldn't believe the condition of the American POWs. McDowell related the story after we were reunited at Ranshofen. "He ordered the German guards to disarm, then looked the other way when some of our POWs took their guns, escorted the guards out of the colonel's sight and shot some of them."

"I'm glad I wasn't there, Mac," I replied. "There's been enough killing, and shooting those guards isn't going to make anything better."

Ranshofen is a small Austrian village, on the east bank of the Salzach River. There, Comer joined back up with Charlie and myself. The liberated flyers were quartered in a deserted steel plant with a concrete floor as a bed. We managed quite well after getting deloused, a shower and clean uniforms. In addition, we got clean blankets and army rations to fill our stomachs. Sleep came easily, especially with a column of American tanks parked outside.

A day later, on April 30, 1945, about 5,000 of us were watching a USO show. "Hitler is confirmed dead," the announcement blared over the loudspeaker. Everyone clapped and cheered and hugged each other. As the talk of an eminent German surrender spread throughout the crowd, tears of joy ran down my face. It was the first and only time during the entire war that I cried.

"I wonder where Father Kane is, Charlie. We need to tell him that those broken wings of ours are about to be mended."

Within the week the former POWs, now American flyers again, were flown back across Germany to northwest France and the small town of Epinal. Crossing the border, between France and Germany, we flew over the Rhine River. We were just south of Solingen. Charlie joked about crossing the Rhine on our descent into Epinal. "The last time I saw that river from the air, we got our butts shot off!"

Once in France we really started to enjoy our newfound freedom. "Before doing anything, you must check where your assigned quarters are located and complete your medical checkup, then you may proceed to the mess hall," the lieutenant told us on arrival. I weighed in at one hundred twenty pounds, fifty less than the day the *Belle* was shot down. Charlie and Cecil had lost a lot of weight as well.

"I'm having steak and eggs," Charlie said on our way out of the medical compound. However, we were put on a soft diet of bread, bread pudding and potato soup with real pieces of Spam. It was the army's way of nursing us back to health.

Charlie was staring into his bowl. "I can't believe they're feeding us soup, the same thing the Krauts gave us in Stalag."

"I'm not inviting Ike to my house for dinner," I said.

"Me either," Charlie added.

"Anybody find any eyes?" Comer asked, tasting his first spoonful.

"Hey, this soup's not half bad!" Charlie announced.

"Charlie," I said.

"Yeah."

"The bread's fresh too. Taste like they made it this morning." I had forgotten how good fresh bread was, especially with butter on it. "Pudding's pretty good too."

When's the last time we had bread pudding?" Cecil asked.

"What the hell," Charlie said, as he ate his pudding. "Ike can come over for dinner."

"Yeah. What the hell," I said. "Besides, he did send someone to come and get us."

"Let's get a seconds," Comer said. We all headed for another helping when Cecil suddenly stopped in his tracks.

"What you doin' Cecil?" I had run into him from the back.

"Just thinking." Cecil's thoughts had drifted back to the prison camp. He was looking at the short line of American soldiers eager to get another helping and the abundance of food. "Remember in Stalag when the chow tub had to be spread out between one hundred thirty-six men, one dipper to a man?"

Army food at Epinal might not have been steak and eggs but it was an awfully good and we got as much as we wanted to eat.

A few days later, the three of us boarded a train and were sent one hundred eighty miles south to St. Vallier and Camp Lucky Strike. After arriving there we got news of Germany's unconditional surrender on May 7. The next day was declared VE day. The camp's commandant gave briefings over the PA each morning. "The first group to be shipped home will be the be the sick and wounded. Next, the RAMPS (Recovered American Military Personnel) will follow in alphabetical order."

"That's us!" Cecil exclaimed. "We'll be back to the States within the week!" We were among the several million GIs who were trying to make their way back home.

Two weeks later, with only one thought on our minds and the RAMPS still not on their way home, we decided to look for our own transportation. That day a DC-3 landed on the airstrip at Camp Lucky Strike and on the tail was the letter "A." The letter "A" identified the ship as part of the First Wing of the 8th Air Force, the same wing that the 401st Bombardment Group was in.

"Hey," Charlie said. "There's our ride to England."

The officer flying this ship was none other than Major, now Colonel Arnold, commander of our group at Madras, Oregon. He had just got to the hanger when the three of us caught up to him.

"Colonel, I believe we were at Madras together in '43." I gave him a short version of the happenings over the last year and a half and said that we were most anxious to get back to Bassingbourn and catch a flight back to the States. "We've been looking for a way back home.

First thing we got to do is get to England. Any chance you might fly us there?"

"Sorry," he said. "Command does not allow pilots the privilege to allocate the destination of military personnel," he added, sounding very much the officer. "But," he continued after a short pause, "my plane is presently anchored in D-36 and is scheduled to depart in fifteen minutes. There is no assigned cargo for the return flight."

Charlie, Cecil and I looked at each other and didn't say a thing when Colonel Arnold went into headquarters to complete his paper work. We headed directly to bay D-36 and took comfortable seats in the back of the DC-3. Without acknowledging who was on board, he went out of his way to return us to Bassingbourn. After landing, we taxied to the far end of the airfield, opposite the main hanger and headquarters.

"Thanks," I said after the short ride back to England. Even Colonel Arnold had a smile on his face as he shook our hands.

"Good luck getting home," he said and headed off across the airfield.

Charlie, Cecil and I just stood there, staring at the huge American airbase.

"It's quite a sight isn't it, Charlie?" I said surveying the airfield. It was our original base at Bassingbourn. Air traffic was as busy as it had been on December 1, 1943, when we last took off from that field.

The three of us then made our way to headquarters. The place was hopping, with everyone scurrying about with post-war assignments. "Sorry, Sarg," the corporal at the desk said. "It's impossible to schedule anyone else on the transport list because it has already been made up for other ground personnel. As a result all planes are full and the load list has already been sent back to Washington. You guys need to check out the squadron bulletin board for openings that come up for transportation. Check for social functions while you're at it."

"That's a kick in the butt," Charlie said, "I thought we were on our way home."

What a surprise: the squadron bulletin board had our names posted as honored guests at the evening dinner and celebration. "Colonel Arnold must have made the arrangements," I told Charlie and Cecil.

What a time it was. The whole camp seemed to be there, many of whom hadn't yet heard the stories about Stalag 17B. The food was terrific and included roast beef, boiled potatoes and ice cream for dessert. The fellowship was equally fantastic even though there wasn't anyone who had been stationed at Bassingbourn the same time we were.

"You guys don't know how good it is to be back here and eating this chow," I told them. They thought that was funny. "I'll never complain about army cooking again!" They thought that was funny too. The three of us were very accommodating, telling different groups over and over about the ordeal that we had been through.

The next morning it was off to see the squadron's commanding officer. He called us into his office, then he too apologized for not being able to fly us back to the States. "I know you guys want out of here," he said. "We're moving troops back to the States as fast as possible. Take this notice to the finance officer and he'll advance each of you $250.00. You'll at least have some spending money while the army continues to try and find some way for you to get home. We'll get you guys back sooner or later."

"It shouldn't be that hard for them to find us a ride home here," Charlie said. "Let's head for London and live it up while they work on transportation."

In London we checked in at the Red Cross Center, "Rainbow Corners."

"There shouldn't be any difficulty in cutting through the red tape and getting you soldiers on your way to the States in short order," the man at the desk said authoritatively, but he couldn't tell us how or when. The Red Cross did find lodging for us at ten shillings a day in a very nice hotel. It looked like it was up to us to find a way to rejoin our families back home. We had sent postal cards home from Bassingbourn but it was anyone's guess when our families would get them.

For the next three weeks Charlie, Cecil and I lived it up, seeing the sights of bombed-out London, attending USO shows and visiting pubs while we fought the war all over again. All the partying burned a hole in our pockets. Our money ran out fast.

Finally, I came up with another idea. "I know how to get home. We'll go right to the top, see Ambassador Winant, explain what's happened and ask him for some help."

"That's pretty funny, Ras," Charlie said. "Just like we're going to get in to see him. Charlie changed his mind when I told him what had happened in Dulag Luft and how I had gotten to know the Ambassador's son.

The next morning, June 18, 1945, the three of us headed for the American Embassy and asked for an audience with Ambassador Winant. The colonel at the information desk wasn't too sure the three sergeants in front of him were playing with full decks until I mentioned how I had met the Ambassador's son. He reluctantly left the confines of his stuffed chair and conveyed the message. It was a few moments later when he returned, led by Ambassador Winant.

"Where are the people who know my son?" the Ambassador asked. The three of us stood up. "Come into my office."

"I met your son one cold night in December of '43. It was under a building at Dulag Luft interrogation center," I told the Ambassador. I finished up the story telling him that despite what the Nazis were trying to get him to say, his son had stayed strong.

"Thank you, Sergeant," he said. "John told me about that night, said he liked you. Right now he is in Switzerland aiding recovered allied prisoners on their way home." The Ambassador was a proud man. His son had made him more proud. "Is there anything I can do for you?"

"In fact there is," I answered in my most diplomatic way. You would have thought that three of us all had rehearsed the answer because we stated in unison, "we want to go home!"

The Ambassador grinned, then conferred with his aide, who produced a business card, which the Ambassador signed. "If you take this card to Watford and present it to the officer in charge, he will arrange a safe trip home for you. Our office will contact them before your arrival. Thank you again for helping John," he said shaking all our hands. Ambassador Winant always remained one of my heroes of the war.

On arrival at Watford we were escorted to the camp's headquarters. "This is great, Charlie." I said. "We're back in Watford. I wonder if they're going to send us to Liverpool next and put us on a ship to Belfast. It looks like we're going home the same route we got here!"

The captain in charge was summoned. I presented the card and gave him our reason for being there. Doubt would be a mild description for the sneer held on his preppy looking face. You could tell by the way he carried himself that he had never seen combat. "Why don't you three go to the barracks and get a shave and shower. You can go to the day center on base for a sandwich and beer. By that time I should have an answer for you." The captain must have gotten an earful from the embassy because we weren't in the barracks for ten minutes when he appeared at a brisk pace. "You will be leaving within the next twenty-four hours," the captain said, "and if there is anything I can do to keep you comfortable, I will be more than happy to do so."

"Well, we would like to visit Bournemouth rather than wait around another army camp. We've been doing that for the last couple of months," I said, stretching the truth just a little. Bournemouth was located on the English Channel southwest of London. According to a brochure I had read, it was the Miami Beach of England. "Can you arrange a visit there while we wait for orders to depart?" I asked. By now the captain had become a gracious host.

"If you gentlemen will proceed to headquarters when you have finished cleaning up, there will be a car and driver waiting. When you arrive in Bournemouth check at the Red Cross Center for any messages from me," the captain told us. Driving in England was slow and methodical. It took a good three hours to get the eighty or so miles from the camp at Watford to the Red Cross Center at Bournemouth. When we arrived, our driver was already being paged.

Charlie, Cecil and I never got the chance to see Bournemouth. "I'm supposed to take you guys immediately to Plymouth," the driver said. Plymouth is another port city in Southern England, one hundred twenty miles west of Bournemouth. So we were back in the car for another four-hour drive. Upon arrival we were instructed to board a LST for our trip home. An LST is a transport ship, some large enough to transport tanks and bulldozers. This one was quite small, no more than a hundred fifty feet long and shaped like a box. It carried one hundred passengers destined to have the ride of their lives along with four Jeeps. After being on board an hour the LST moved out. Ambassador Winant had promised us a ride home within twenty-four hours and he did just that.

"They must be transporting us to a larger ship out in the harbor for our trip to the States," Charlie said. We all went topside to see what naval vessel we would be docking up with. But that never happened. As the LST moved out of the harbor we passed subs, destroyers, battlewagons and carriers. Cruising speed was nine knots. In heavy seas the LST come to a complete stop. I think, at times, the ship went backwards. Not being a sailor at heart, I stayed in the sack for most of the first three days. Ten days after leaving Plymouth, on June 28, 1945, the LST docked at the large naval station at Newport News, Virginia. There was little fanfare at Newport News. A lot of GIs had been returning home during the two months since we had escaped from the Leach Forest.

The first thing I did was call my family, then went to headquarters for debriefing. After that, Charlie, Cecil and I picked up our orders. Orders put us on indefinite leave but said that we would be notified if we were required to return for further assignment. That gave me quite a pause. We were issued train tickets to our hometowns. Mine was for a two-day ride to Detroit, leaving on June 30, where I would transfer to another train to Traverse City. It had been over three years since I had been at the recruiting station in Detroit.

"A lot has happened since we flew out of Gander two years ago, huh Ras?" Charlie said when we got to the train station.

"Keep in touch," I told him, and gave him a quick salute as I boarded the iron horse.

It was quiet on the train to Detroit. Never in the past three years had any day passed as slowly as the three days it took to get home. I sat there lost in my private thoughts. There were no more bombing runs, no more days as a POW living day to day. Soon things would be normal again. I'd be home and see my family. Harry and I will have fun again. I'll finish college and get a job.

On a warm and sunny July afternoon, just after five o'clock, the train rolled into Traverse City. It was the happiest moment of my life. I was just one month shy of my twenty-fifth birthday. Mom and Dad met me at the station. Mom had tears in her eyes. She gave me a big hug and a kiss.

"Welcome home, Sarg," Dad said, shaking my hand with a smile on his face.

On September 17, 1945, I was honorably discharged from military service of the United States of America. With the orders came quite a grubstake, seventeen months of back pay, flyers pay at that! The Air Force ponied up for all the time that I had spent as a POW in Stalag. Along with the money that I had sent home before going overseas, I felt rich!

Epilogue

AFTER THE WAR, THE UNITED STATES 8TH AIR FORCE decorated Sergeant William Rasmussen and the other crewmembers of the *Hell's Belle* with several medals. Bill received the European, African, Middle Eastern Medal with four bronze stars, the American Campaign Medal, the Air Medal, the POW Medal, the WWII Victory Medal and the Good Conduct Medal.

Over the years, a number of the crew of the *Hell's Belle* got together for reunions. In addition to Bill, Charles Dyer, Cecil Comer, Charles Quinn, Gerald McDowell and Bert Steiler all took part. The last one was held in 1988.

On October 27, 1998, over fifty years after the war ended, but not one day forgotten, America lost one of the good guys. Bill passed away following a long illness. Reverends Father Patrick Barrett, Fr. James Gardiner and Fr. William Lipscomb served as celebrants for a Funeral Mass that was celebrated at St. Francis Catholic Church in Traverse City, Michigan. I listened as Father Barrett, the Irish Catholic priest who played golf with my dad over the years, gave the eulogy. When the congregation sang, *"He will raise you up on eagles wings, bear you on the breath of dawn . . ."* I wondered if those in the congregation knew that He had already done that, over fifty years earlier, at dawn, on another set of wings. How ironic, I thought, that back then it was a different bird of prey, the *Hell's Belle*. I think that the Good Lord was always with my dad.

Bill was laid to rest with full military honors at St. Joseph Catholic Cemetery in Mapleton just outside Traverse City. Graveside services were held under the auspices of the Veterans of Foreign Wars, Cherryland Post No. 2780. With the Veterans standing at attention, the American flag that draped the coffin was folded and handed to my Mom. When the coffin was lowered into the grave the honor guard fired a fifteen-gun salute to honor the fallen soldier.

About William E. Rasmussen

THIS BOOK WAS BASED ON THE MEMOIRS OF WILLIAM E. Rasmussen, "From a B-17 to Stalag 17B." Some of the characters are fictional. Bill was a sergeant in the United States Air Force during WWII. He became a ball turret operator and gunner on the B-17 Flying Fortresses including the *Anxious Angel*, the *"079" Buccaneer* and the *Hell's Belle*. Bill was assigned to the 401st Bombardment Squadron of the 91st Bomb Group of the 8th Air Force that flew out of Bassingbourn, England. This story is about Bill's personal account of military training, combat missions aboard the B-17 and the time he spent as a prisoner of war.

Bill dedicated his memoirs to his wife Norma, his children, Margaret, William, Randall, Beth Marie and Rebecca, to the crew of the *Hell's Belle* and to all of the men and women of our armed forces that gave their lives so that the rest of us could live as a free people.

In 1946 Bill married Norma McManus and returned to complete his degree at Central Michigan Teachers College now Central Michigan University. Following college Bill had a career with Firestone Tire and Rubber Company, Mapleton Garage, Inc. and the National Bank and Trust Company in Traverse City, Michigan. For fun he played trumpet in the *Riverboat Six*, a Dixieland Band.

APPENDIX I

The B-17 and the American Flyer

WWII was the second major war in the industrial age. As such, it was the second war that employed fighter and bomber aircraft. American aircraft engineering and aviation industry changed the "flying coffins" of WWI into "the wings of war" of WWII, highly effective combat aircraft that demanded the respect from their fiercest enemy. It was the first time in the history of warfare that efficient, yet combat worthy craft were used. WWII was the first time that such a massive and devastating role was played in such an effective manner by one aircraft, the B-17, against such a fortified enemy, Nazi Germany and its occupied countries in Western Europe.

The B-17 was born in a Boeing factory on July 17, 1935, originally as the B-229, and subsequently designated by the Air Force as the XB-17. Development of the B-229 was based on a strategic assumption that if invasion came to American shores, it would come by sea. The planners of weapon development made a tactical decision to design a long-range, land-based bomber that could attack and destroy enemy aircraft carriers and transport ships long before they reached American beaches. It was a reporter who dubbed the B-17 a "Fortress" that would defend our coastline. The B-17 became known as the "Queen of the Sky."

From an engineering standpoint, the Flying Fortress was a powerful four-engine heavy bomber, the "B" connoting bomber. After turbo-superchargers and a fireproof fuel line system were added, the XB-17 became known as the Y1B-17A, history's first stratospheric bomber. In 1939, Boeing engineers changed the belly gun position from inside the ship to inside a sphere (a "ball turret" that rotated 360 degrees), and placed it underneath the ship. Subsequent improvements were identified alphabetically after the 17, such as adding a chin-turret and designating it the B-17G. The crews were proud of her capability, reliability and endurance. Compared to the B-24 Liberator, the B-17 could fly higher by 5,000 feet, was easier to control and was better in combat. B-17 flyers used to joke that the Liberator was "the crate that the Fortress was shipped in." Unlike the B-24 Liberator, the B-17s wings could be hit by enemy fire and not fold, hydraulic lines had to be damaged in more than one place to incapacitate the B-17.

The British began bombing runs against Germany in 1939. The B-17A first went to war as a result of the Lend-Lease Act signed March 11, 1941 and was flown by British pilots. It struck targets in Germany as well as Nazi convoys on the Mediterranean Sea. In the summer of 1942, America's assault on Fortress Europe began with its daylight bombing campaign, complimenting the existing night bombing by the British. No one at that Boeing plant in 1935 had ever imagined that America, in 1942, would begin to base thousands of these ships in southern England and that they would be in a fight for Britain and America's survival. The B-17, then later in the war the B-24, became the workhorses of the 8th Air Force. In total, the USAF placed 12,597 B-17 combat aircraft over the skies of Europe (including 512 B-17Es, 3,400 B-17Fs and 8,685 B-17Gs), and an additional 18,000 B-24 Liberators. 6,562 of these aircraft were lost in operations. The average life of a B-17 in combat was mere fifty days.

Once America was in the war, the B-17's designated function was "daylight precision bombing." The USAF had developed the Norden bombsight that enabled the bombardier to "flip a dime into a pickle barrel from 10,000 feet." This automatic flight control device onboard the B-17 provided the link between the bombardier and the aircraft's automatic pilot. With it, the bombardier was able to coordinate the variables of airspeed, direction, altitude, air resistance, wind and target motion for the first time in aviation history.

With a crew of ten and a range of 2,800 miles, the B-17 carried enough fuel to leave the shores of England, deliver its payload deep into Germany and return to its base in England. The B-17 had a cruising speed of 302 MPH that decreased to 155 MPH for the bombing run, its most vulnerable portion during the sortie. Over Germany, the B-17 flew without fighter escort. The American P-38 Lighting and P-47 Thunderbolt ("The Jug") fighter's range were limited to only 600 miles. Even the P-51 Mustang fighter had limited range until its fuel tanks were modified in mid-1944. The B-17F's armor consisted of eleven .50-caliber Browning machine guns, two in the top turret, two in back, one each for the bombardier, navigator and radio operator, one for each waist gunner, and two in the ball turret beneath the ship, high caliber guns that gave it the capability to defend itself from the German Messerschmitt Bf-109s, 110s and 210s, and Focke Wulf 190A-8s.

The role of the B-17 was to help destroy the German war machine and bomb the German military and civilian population into submission. Its mission was completed very efficiently and very successfully. The 8th Air Force selected targets to destroy Germany's capacity for making war. Targets selected included aircraft factories used to produce the Messerschmitt and Focke Wulf fighters. Shipbuilding sites and naval bases, including U-boat installations, were high on the target list. Power stations, and oil installations, when destroyed, helped cripple the enemy. Industrial targets such as the Bavarian Motors Works (BMW), Daimler-Benz, and the Linde Oxygen Factory became primary targets. Railroads moved the German machinery. They, as well as rail marshalling yards were selected. Ball bearings allow machines to move; factories that produced them were destroyed. Seats of government, including Munich and Berlin, made the list. We were assigned to destroy a cutlery factory, located in the Rhine Country and converted to make bayonets. It was an assignment that proved fateful to our ship, the *Hell's Belle*.

B-17s pounded the German war machine mercilessly. By the time Germany surrendered, American aircraft dropped over 700,000 tons of bombs (along with 950,000 tons dropped by the RAF), fired ninety-nine million rounds of ammunition, and destroyed 95% of rail transportation, fuel generating capacity and other core components needed by the Germans to wage a modern war. There simply was nothing left for the Nazis to manufacture the products of war. By the end of the war, coordinated strikes allowed over a 1,000 aircraft to attack a designated target in a single raid. The "strategic bombing" campaign creating an "internal blockade" on the Germans, a self-sustaining blockade that weakened the perimeter of Nazi held European Theater, weakening it for the eventual ground invasion by the Allied forces. The bombing campaign, waged so effectively against the Nazis, lowered the cost of lives of our invading ground forces. By war's end, the strategic bombing campaign resulted in German armies being isolated because of communication failures, lack of ammunition and supplies.

Hermann Goering, the German Air Force chief, boasted that he would become "a flying Dutchman" before the Allies controlled the sky over Nazi occupied Europe. Goering had assured Hitler that "the shadow of an enemy plane shall never fall on Nazi Germany." Despite his boast, the 8th Air Force, along with the RAF, eventually wrestled control of the European sky from the German Luftwaffe. By the end of the war the Allies referred to the air sirens sounding in German occupied cities as "the Dutchman blowing his horn." Between the summer of 1942 and the time of Germany's unconditional surrender on May 8, 1945, American and RAF bombing missions continued into the heart of Nazi Empire. Forty-five thousand tons of bombs were dropped in the three hundred sixty-three missions flown against Berlin alone. The B-17s' shadows must have been seen in Hitler's nightmares. Even Goering had to know that the German fate was sealed when he saw the P-51 Mustang escorting the heavy bombers in raids over Berlin. German residential areas were also devastated with a staggering loss of civilian life, an estimated 305,000 in all. Incendiary and high explosive bombing that lasted nine days, in July and August 1943, devastated Hamburg. An estimated 50,000 civilians died, nearly the same number that died in all of England in all the war. When Dresden was destroyed in February 1945, 35,000 German civilians died. One unforeseen result of this was the vengeance that was taken out on the captured American and British flyers. Despite the Geneva Convention and the recognized rules of war governing captured soldiers, the civilian population killed many of the captured American flyers. German soldiers and civilians shot flyers as they parachuted from their stricken craft.

One German writer described the American bombing campaign waged against Nazi Germany as "wasteful, inhumane, and ineffective." However, the Nazis proved, beyond any doubt, that their conquest was intended to lead them to complete domination of all people and destruction of any country that stood in their way. They had grossly miscalculated America's capacity to wage war. The American aviation industry had developed a Flying Fortress, complemented by American flyers that were every bit as lethal and every move as destructive as anything that the Nazis had ever produced. The B-17 proved to be an American answer to German aggression.

The captured American flyers were brave and determined. They fought the air battles over Europe, at times until their planes were shot from underneath them, hung onto shreds of flaming aircraft, and continued to fight on. With determination, they inflicted great losses on the enemy until there was nothing left with which to fight. They jumped or crash-landed in a strange and hostile country, only to start the battle for survival all over again. With fear, starvation, cold temperatures and a hostile civilian population as their constant companions, these airmen struggled to keep their health and sanity as they tried to get home. With determination and hope accompanying them in the German prison camps, they continued to help one another when all seemed lost. The American flyers were willing to suffer beyond the call of duty for the principles of freedom.

If it had not been through the combined efforts of the armored units, infantry, paratroopers, marines, sailors, coastguard, seabees, all the supporting forces, plus the people at home and our allies, America would never have succeeded. All the flyers were extremely proud and thankful for their support. Without their efforts, the captured flyers would never have made it home.

APPENDIX II

The 8th Air Force and Daylight Bombing

In the autumn of 1939, Luftwaffe bombing preceded the German blitzkrieg into Poland. Stuka dive-bombers struck their Polish targets with relative impunity from the minimal Polish air defenses. For RAF bombers, in the fall of 1939, bombing German targets was a different story. Attacking German military installations during daylight resulted in significant RAF losses. The German air defenses, including antiaircraft batteries and fighter planes, inflicted heavy losses on the RAF bombers. The loss of bombers led the British to abandon daylight bombing in favor of night bombing. Diminished navigation became an accepted downside to the edge in defense that bombing at night provided. The British heavy bombers stealthily crept through the German night skies, streaming one behind the other. In order to protect their aircraft, the Germans too converted to night bombing, allowing the darkness to provide an added measure of protection. They had learned the lessons of daylight air battles. With the dawn of night bombing, the air war opened a new chapter.

The Americans, who entered the war at the end of 1941, adhered to a doctrine of "precision daylight bombing." It was their official policy in the spring of 1942 when the 8th Air Force took over airfields in southeast England. On July 4, 1942, the Americans flew their first bombing mission against German occupied airfields in Holland. On August 17, 1942, for the first time, American flyers flew the B-17 in combat. American daylight bombing campaign over Fortress Europe had commenced. In the initial months the 17s flew a limited number of short-range missions into France, Holland and Belgium with fighter escort, all during daylight. At the end of 1942, a mere twenty-seven USAF combat missions had been flown.

In January 1943, in a luxurious villa outside of Casablanca on the northern coast of Morocco, Roosevelt and Churchill agreed on a strategic plan of bombing Germany before invasion, "Operation Point Blank." General Hap Arnold, Chief of the USAF was there, as was General Ira Eaker, Commander of the 8th Air Force. It was at this juncture in the war that round the clock bombing of Germany was endorsed. The directive given to Eaker was, "progressive destruction and dislocation of the German military, industrial and economic system and the undermining of the morale of the German people to a point where their capacity for armed resistance was fatally weakened."

On January 27, 1943, on the northern coast of Germany, a submarine building center at Wilhelmshaven became the first target for American bombers on German soil. The P-38 Lighting and P-47 Thunderbolt provided fighter escort. Four months after American crews flew the B-17 against Fortress Europe, bombing of the Fatherland had begun.

Shortly after, in the summer of 1943, and a year after the first bombing missions against airbases in Holland, the Americans began testing a new policy of long range bombing without fighter escort. For the first time the American bombing was extended to the interior of Germany, a country fortified with antiaircraft installations and German fighters, and battle hardened from the British sorties flown against them. Stalin wanted American and British troops to invade Germany in a ground assault. Roosevelt and Churchill had disagreed. British and American policy was set. The fight against Fortress Europe, from the west, came first from the sky.

Four wings made the 1st Air Division of the 8th Air Force. Each wing consisted of three bombardment groups. Each bombardment group had four squadrons. On any given day, six planes from each squadron were assigned to the mission and an additional B-17 was assigned as a backup in case of mechanical failure of one of the primary planes. It was also assigned in case crewmembers from one of the primary ships had been injured or killed on the previous raid.

Each squadron had twenty-five to forty ships available for assignment; an assignment that for any given ship and crew came, on average, every four days. The bombardment groups had an additional thirty to forty B-17s in reserve. The reserve ships continuously replaced lost B-17s thus allowing the squadrons to keep a full compliment of aircraft. The *Buccaneer*, the first B-17 Rasmussen's crew flew in combat, a ship from the 401st Squadron of the 91st Bombardment Group of the 1st Air Wing, was classified lost on November 26, 1943. The *Hell's Belle*, the last B-17 Rasmussen's crew flew in combat, was transferred from the 385th to the 401st Squadron, in the 91st Bombardment Group of the 1st Air Wing. The *Belle* and her crew were classified lost on December 1, 1943.

Unlike the British bombers that shadowed each other in a stream as they flew through the German night skies, the B-17s formed at dawn at rendezvous points over the North Sea; six planes from each of the four squadrons, twenty-four ships from each of the three bombardment groups, seventy-two B-17s in a vertical wedge. It was Colonel Curtis E. "Iron Ass" LeMay, a thirty-five year old Ohioan who commanded the 305th Bombardment Group, of the 40th Air Wing, of the 1st Air Division, that designed the attack formation. Multiple vertical wedges rendezvoused over the North Sea, all in attack formation as the ships flew towards their primary target; each wedge stacked 1,000 feet above or below the other.

The combat wing provided the maximum protection from the German fighters, especially from frontal assaults. The armament of the B-17 along with the vertical wedge, were believed to provide enough protection without fighter escort for the heavy bombers to fly sorties into the heart of Germany during daylight, a policy that resulted in a staggering loss of American warships and flyers. Walter Cronkite, a war correspondent at the time and an observer on one of the early bombing missions, described the B-17 bombing missions as "an assignment to hell—a hell 26,000 feet above the earth."

On July 25, 1943, the Allies began the attack on Hamburg in what the American flyers called "blitzweek." Hamburg was turned into a firestorm. With it came the loss of eighty-seven B-17s. Loss of American bombers on a given mission climbed from an "acceptable" 3.6% to 6.4%. Three hundred thirty B-17s began bombing runs that week from their English bases. At week's end only two hundred were left. Nine hundred American flyers had been killed, wounded or captured in a single week. General Eaker gave a short reprieve to flights deep inside Germany because of the alarming loss of B-17s and their crews.

Three weeks later, on August 16, 1943, the order was given to bomb ball bearing factory at Schweinfurt in the center of Germany and a Messerschmitt factory at Regensburg in southeast Germany, near the Bavarian Forest. On the morning of August 17, 1943, three hundred eighty B-17s departed two hours late because of cloud cover and arrived over Germany without fighter escort, the short-range fighters having turned back before the German border. The two waves split, one wing flying south to Schweinfurt, the second southeast to Regensburg. By days end a total sixty ships were shot down, a 16% loss of American bombers on a single raid. Five hundred fifty flyers were missing in action and presumed dead or captured. These staggering losses led to a drop in moral and confidence among the flyers that eventually led to a change in USAF fighter escort policy.

America's P-51 Mustang, available since October 1940, was powered with one 1,490-HP Rolls-Royce/Packard Merlin engine, was thirty-two feet long, had a wingspan of thirty-seven feet and had a maximum speed of 437 MPH at 25,000 feet. It had a crew of one. Its armament consisted of six .50-caliber Browning machine guns. The fighter had already been modified by the British for additional fuel capacity but had been dismissed by the USAF as too susceptible to fire until it was again modified in the cockpit and retrofitted for additional fuel capacity. Its radius was extended to nine hundred fifty miles, enough to extend its a range to Berlin and back. In mid-1944 the USAF placed it into service as a long-range fighter, the P-51D. The effect was immediate.

In March 1943, twenty-five combat missions got a flyer a ground assignment, or a job as an instructor; maybe the flyer even got to go home. In April, the number was raised to thirty, more than the entire number of missions flown by the USAF in 1942. By May 1942, the number of combat crews of the 8th Air Force stationed in England increased from one hundred to two hundred twenty-five. By the end of 1942, seven hundred twenty B-17s and B-24 Liberators could leave their English bases on a single raid. By 1944 crews for the heavy bombers again became harder to come by than the ships they flew, and the number of combat missions needed to get a ground assignment was raised to thirty-five.

The United States Air Force policy of daylight bombing continued until the last day of the war.

Printed in the United States
35185LVS00003B/565-588